The Bitter Taste of Hope

SUNY series in New Political Science

Bradley J. Macdonald, editor

The Bitter Taste of Hope

Ideals, Ideologies, and Interests in the Age of Obama

Stephen Eric Bronner

SUNY PRESS

Published by State University of New York Press, Albany

Printed in the United States of America

For information, contact State University of New York Press, Albany, NY
www.sunypress.edu

Production, Ryan Morris
Marketing, Michael Campochiaro

Library of Congress Cataloging-in-Publication Data

Names: Bronner, Stephen Eric, 1949– author.
Title: The bitter taste of hope : ideals, ideologies, and interests in the age of Obama / Stephen Eric Bonner.
Description: Albany : State University of New York Press, 2017. | Series: SUNY series in new political science | Includes bibliographical references and index.
Identifiers: LCCN 2016031495 (print) | LCCN 2016050551 (ebook) | ISBN 9781438465494 (hardcover : alk. paper) | ISBN 9781438465487 (pbk : alk. paper) | ISBN 9781438465500 (e-book)
Subjects: LCSH: Obama, Barack. | United States—Politics and government—2009– | United States—Foreign relations—2009– | United States—Foreign relations—Middle East. | Middle East—Foreign relations—United States.
Classification: LCC E907.B76 2017 (print) | LCC E907 (ebook) | DDC 973.932092—dc23
LC record available at https://lccn.loc.gov/2016031495

10 9 8 7 6 5 4 3 2 1

Rosalyn Baxandall,

feminist, intellectual, activist—and comrade

Contents

Acknowledgments

There are always many people to thank for helping bring a book to fruition. Bradley Macdonald suggested that I put together this volume for the fine series he is editing for SUNY Press, and Manfred Steger was just as enthusiastic about the project. I owe an extraordinary debt to Dr. James Jennings and Cliff Gardner of Conscience International and US Academics for Peace with whom I traveled for various efforts in civic diplomacy to Iran, Iraq, Palestine, Sudan/Darfur, and Syria. Along with friends like Janet Amighi and Lawrence Davidson, they helped expand my world and, through their humanitarian commitments, attempt to turn theory into practice. I also owe a debt to my colleagues, Alex Hinton and Nela Navarro, at the Center for the Study of Genocide and Human Rights at Rutgers University. Lastly, I would like to thank a group of doctoral students who worked with me and who provided excellent comments in a seminar about the manuscript. These fine scholars include: Aaron Kraut, Kelsey Lizotte, Barea Sinno, David Staszheim, Sarah Weirich, and especially my principal research assistant Edwin Daniel Jacob whose support was invaluable. And then, of course, there is my wife Anne Burns, who has always supported my work as she has shared my travels.

Chapter 2 is based on an invited talk for the Swedish Association of Sciences in 2009 and chapter 8 on a lecture for the International Forum on the Holocaust at the Russian State University in Moscow, also in 2015. Chapters 1, 4, 16, 19, 21, 22, and 27 initially appeared whole or in part in *Logos: A Journal of Modern Society and Culture*, www.logosjournal.com. Chapters 3, 6, 10, 11, 12, 13, 14, 17, 18, 19, 20, 23, 25, and 26 appeared whole or in part in *Reader Supported News*, www.rsnorg.org. Chapter 5 initially appeared in the *Green European Journal*, and chapters 7 and 15 in the Heathwood Press, www.heathwoodpress.com. Chapter 24 initially appeared in the *Tehran Times*.

Introduction

Obama's Legacy

Composed of popular essays and articles written between 2008 and 2016, which mostly appeared in Internet journals, *The Bitter Taste of Hope* starts where my previously published books *Blood in the Sand* and *Peace Out of Reach* left off. Soaring hopes raised by the presidential victory of Barack Obama soon shared the public sphere with surging racism, gun violence, cultural conflicts, religious extremism, attacks on past reforms, rising intolerance and xenophobia, and manifold fears of democracy and modernity. Some essays in this volume were inspired by impressions of what was transpiring, others by forgotten tragedies, still others by memories, but most of all by the subaltern's attempts to (using the famous phrase of C. Wright Mills) "translate private troubles into public issues." I visited many of the places that I wrote about in this book, and my work in civic diplomacy was complemented by some degree of involvement in political action here at home. There also is a personal touch to this collection (as there was to the prequels) but, this time, I included a few interviews that highlight the connection between scholarship and practice.

The Bitter Taste of Hope is not *about* Barack Obama but rather certain ideals and principles, practices and policies, that congealed during the years of his presidency. It investigates not only American involvement in Afghanistan and Iraq, the Israeli-Palestinian conflict and foreign policy toward Iran, but the national hopes of Circassians and the suffering endured by the "garbage people" of Cairo. *The Bitter Taste of Hope* also treats the Arab Spring and the ensuing international counter-revolution less in terms particular to the Orient than through their structural dynamics. The Middle East has been deeply impacted by the West and, most particularly, by American actions in the region. Its invasions and failed attempts at nation-building in Afghanistan and Iraq paved the way for civil war in Afghanistan and Iraq, the devolution of Syria, the catastrophic Libyan intervention, and the rise of ISIS. An idealistic belief in its democratic "mission," fortified by crude realism predicated on the end justifying the means, also led the United States to ally with the most hated nations in the region (such as Bahrain, Israel, and Saudi Arabia), thereby identifying it with lack of respect for international law, hypocritical policies on human rights, employment of the double standard, and imperialist ambitions.

Old grievances among the exploited and disenfranchised remained unaddressed even while transnational uprisings embracing enlightenment and often utopian ideals battled counter-revolutionary movements inspired by authoritarian and dogmatic religious values. Peaceful protest encountered violent response during the Green Revolution in Iran, the short-lived Egyptian republic, and (of course) Syria. New demands are being placed on American foreign policy even as the dead hand of tradition imperils progress at home and abroad. With that in mind, the structure of this volume is almost self-evident: "Ideals and Interests," the opening section, introduces the norms and themes that shaped the Obama years and retain their salience; "Murderous Impulses," the second section, speaks to certain human tragedies and (seemingly acceptable) irrational attitudes that attack humanitarian values and progressive politics; "Rebellion American Style," meanwhile, illuminates some of the movements and anticipatory themes that inspired American social movements during the Obama presidency; and, finally, "War and Peace," the concluding section, offers some insights into American foreign policy of the past and how it might be transvalued for the future.

Crystallizing the complex of regulative ideals, political dynamics, and cultural norms operative since 2008 is Barack Obama. His successful campaign for the presidency was carried on a wave of hope. A black intellectual and junior senator from Illinois, a graduate of Columbia University and Harvard Law School, who had opposed Hillary Clinton and mainstream Democrats on the invasion of Iraq, he provided a breath of fresh air for a nation suffering from its worst economic implosion since 1929, two worthless imperialist wars, failed conservative domestic policies, and collapse of its international moral standing. Such was the state of political affairs when George W. Bush left office. The real shock should have come when the Republican Party with all that baggage and the worst presidential ticket in recent memory—Senator John McCain (R-AZ) and Governor Sarah Palin (R-AK)—lost by little more than 5 percent of the popular vote to Obama and his vice-presidential running mate, Senator Joe Biden (D-DE). Contrived obstacles to passing budgets and implementing policies, personal insults and affronts occurred from the moment they took office, and disillusionment was inevitable given the unrealistic expectations that had arisen: compromises were (sometimes legitimately) condemned, legislation was (often) considered not radical enough, and new problems emerged where old ones were only partially solved. Nevertheless, I believe, history will view Barack Obama far more favorably than so many of his contemporaries view him.

Rarely has a president been attacked with such ferocity both from the conservative mainstream and the far right. In dialectical terms, the radicalism of Obama and the degree to which his policies were "socialist" are best understood by the counter-revolutionary reaction they fostered. Even on the left, however, radical policies received little enthusiastic support, and timidity marked the stance of moderate "blue dog" Democrats. The day that Obama entered the White House was the day on which Senate Republicans made clear that their sole purpose was to see him fail. They were spurred on by what soon became the Tea Party that would dominate the GOP through 2016, when virtually all its major contenders for the presidency—Donald Trump, Ted Cruz, Marco Rubio, and Ben Carson—reflected the new extremist outlook. Every policy, every proposal, and every executive order became subject to what can only be described as hysterical opposition from Republicans and lukewarm support by conservative Democrats. Without public demonstrations of support from the left, and unanimity within his own party (Obamacare, for example, passed by only one vote in Congress), well-organized right-wing organizations and media like Fox News insisted that President Obama lacked a national mandate. Compromises with large corporations and banks were made, executive orders on immigration, gun regulation, and other issues were often slow in coming, and residues of failed agendas infected much of American foreign policy in the Middle East. Nevertheless, Obama will be remembered for his stand on the "big" issues:

Redirecting foreign policy. The Obama presidency wound down American involvement in the two disastrous wars in Afghanistan and Iraq initiated by the Bush administration. Faced with threats from ISIS, which did not yet exist under his predecessor, Obama reduced battlefield troops from 200,000 in Afghanistan and Iraq combined to 4,087 and 9,800, respectively (*New York Times*, 15 May 2016). That new forms of intervention may result from loosening the rules of engagement by American military personnel remains a real possibility. Claiming credit for killing Osama bin Laden, and thereby bringing symbolic closure to 9/11, Obama did approve airstrikes and drone attacks in Libya, Pakistan, Somalia, and Yemen. For better or worse, his aim was to avoid putting American troops on the ground while debilitating a transnational enemy exemplifying religious barbarism. Obama resisted right-wing pressure for full-scale military intervention in Syria and Ukraine while challenging the doctrine of the preemptive strike and unilateral military action. He will also be remembered as a staunch advocate for international cooperation on dealing with climate change, the Kyoto Protocols, and closing the notorious Guantanamo prison complex. Obama sought to build bridges between nations even as he recognized the importance of how the rest of the world views the United States.

Radicalizing economic policy. Obama's administration pulled the country out of the Great Recession of 2007–2008 and rehabilitated the welfare state. It resisted cuts in programs ranging from social security to food stamps and defended collective bargaining and workers' rights. Obama turned back the economic culture of deregulation and free market capitalism by introducing new regulations on large corporations and big banks (especially through the Dodd-Frank Act of 2010), providing $80 billion to bail out the American auto industry in 2009, creating sixteen million new jobs between 2008 and 2016,[1] updating overtime regulations in 2016 that would immediately benefit four million low-salaried workers,[2] lowering payments on student loans for millions of citizens,[3] raising the minimum wage from $7.25 per hour to $12 per hour in 2020,[4] raising taxes on the top 1 percent by more than 6 percent,[5] and—perhaps above all—passing the Affordable Care Act newly insuring nearly eighteen million citizens.[6] None of this resulted in loss of jobs or slowing of economic growth as conservatives had predicted, and it is fair to say that Obama's domestic agenda was crucial in setting the stage for the explicitly socialist candidacy of Senator Bernie Sanders in 2016.

Defending democracy and changing the culture. Obama defended the state from a right-wing takeover in the election of 2012. His administration protected civil rights and liberties, affirmative action, cultural diversity, and secular attitudes. Initiatives were also begun on neglected issues such as nutrition, obesity, and mental health. Obama used the bully pulpit to excoriate incarceration policies, institutional racism, and lack of gun control legislation. His administration supported abortion rights, same-sex marriage, amnesty for illegal immigrants, Planned Parenthood, and free admission for all students to community colleges. As president, Obama identified with science, reasoned discourse, and a cosmopolitan outlook. His decisions to deal with what were considered rogue states were remarkable: Obama opened relations with Cuba, concluded a nuclear treaty with Iran, and in 2016 became the first sitting president to visit Vietnam and Hiroshima. All of this, in concert with the personal dignity, civility, humor, and cosmopolitan sophistication exhibited by this first black president, gave a jolt to what Marx once termed the "material level of culture."

Each essay in *The Bitter Taste of Hope* provides a fragment for what has become a new worldview initiated during the Obama years. The whole will, I hope, constitute more than the sum of its parts or what Walter Benjamin termed a "constellation" in which the reader can assemble and reassemble its elements in terms of his or her shifting priorities. American policymakers seem unable to think through the failures and mistakes of even the recent past. Enormous pressure was placed on Obama to continue with nation-building in Afghanistan, Libya, and Yemen, send ground troops into Iraq to fight ISIS, and set up a no-fly zone over Syria. These options all reflect the failed thinking and policies of the past. They ignore long-term costs in favor of (possible) short-term gains even as they both misconstrue and underestimate the consequences attendant upon alienated forms of sovereignty. The temptation to intervene is intoxicating, and only a strong dose of political modesty can prevent the United States from becoming enmeshed in yet new proxy wars. Its policymakers have neither the wisdom nor the knowledge to solve every world problem crisis while calls for the government to "do something"—even if has no idea what to do—reflect frustration rather than strategy.

*The Bitter Taste of Hop*e articulates the ways in which burgeoning reactionary values took on dynamics of their own culminating in the astonishing electoral triumph of Donald Trump in the presidential campaign of 2016. President Obama was correct that a straight line connects the nomination of Sarah Palin to the triumph of Donald Trump. But few understood the sheer power of an increasingly acceptable reactionary ideology and even fewer expected that its principal advocate would simply overwhelm Obama's anointed successor, former Secretary of State Hillary Clinton. To be sure, her involvement in what became an overblown and baseless email scandal, the shady dealings of the Clinton Foundation, and (equally baseless) conspiracies of one sort or another had a terrible impact. But an ongoing set of outrageous comments by Donald Trump about a "gold-star" military family, the disabled, women, Mexicans and Muslims built the mistaken confidence of her campaign. Apparently distrust of one candidate vanquished the bigotry of another—and the "experts" were proven wrong.

Liberal media such as MSNBC sought to build ratings by attacking Trump vociferously day after day in a self-satisfied fashion. They provided him millions of dollars in free publicity and air-time forgetting the old publishing adage: "better to be attacked than ignored." Enough voters were also disgusted by the shenanigans of the liberal mainstream, who awarded Clinton over four hundred delegates before the primaries even began, and how the Democratic National Committee led by Congresswoman Debbie Wasserman Schultz and party insiders like Donna Brazile tried to undermine the presidential primary campaign of Bernie Sanders. The "insider" lost to the "outsider." Or, in more sophisticated terms, the rising expectations and popularity of Obama at the end of his presidency produced the rising expectations that, it seemed, Hillary Clinton could not fulfill and that resulted in the counter-revolution of the Tea Party and Donald Trump.

Clinton reflected the right-wing of the Obama presidency. Her insiders sought to highlight her unique political preparation for the highest office, her pragmatism, and the revolutionary impact of having a woman break through the "glass ceiling." But political preparation did not eradicate her "mistake" in supporting the Iraq war, neo-liberal trade treaties like NAFTA, and an interventionist foreign policy. Her pragmatism boiled down to watered down versions of proposals made by more radical Democrats and her campaign overestimated her attraction to white women who chose to vote for their race over their gender—perhaps in part because of the unrelenting sexism of Trump's campaign and in part because race rather than gender provided them with their privileges. Clinton's campaign simply assumed that white workers tied to anachronistic industries in the "rust belt" of the Midwest would vote for her in spite of her neo-liberal commitment to free trade, lackluster class appeal, and neo-liberal commitments to an interventionist foreign policy. But it was ultimately the seven million fewer voters in 2016 that proved decisive: smaller turnout always favors elites, too many rejected the "lesser evil" on symbolic grounds, Clinton could not overcome the apathy of others, and it was clear from the start that she simply lacked the charisma of Bernie Sanders let alone Barack Obama.

Questions have arisen about the president's legacy no less than the need to counter the prevailing apathy and despair. How many of Obama's achievements will vanish during Trump's time in office remains an open question. Whether in foreign or domestic affairs, however, the conflict-ridden and ideologically polarized years of the Obama presidency offer new prospects for furthering progress and democracy. New manifestations of prejudice and police violence, joblessness and despair, brought young people, and especially young people of color, into the street. Valuable social and political reforms from the past have been imperiled, if not rolled back, and counter-revolution still threatens American democracy. With the global impact of every decision becoming ever greater, and with potential genocide always looming, young activists and intellectuals understand that politics is too important to leave in the hands of self-styled experts. This book is meant primarily for them and perhaps also the general reader concerned with the ideologies, ideals, and interests that have been shaping our lives. What is rapidly becoming history can still serve as a teacher, and insofar as all progressives remain responsible for challenging ill-defined geopolitical interests, the need to reflect upon the Obama presidency is more urgent than ever before. *The Bitter Taste of Hope* offers a contribution to that undertaking. I trust that its audience will agree.

Part I

Ideals and Interests

With the election of Barack Obama in 2008, utopian hopes soared. It was believed that the world would change, and perhaps it did as dramatic events occurred that revolved around "rights" and the legacies deriving from the two great political heirs of the Enlightenment: liberalism and socialism. Not so long ago, it was assumed that enlightenment ideals had been domesticated but the Arab Spring of 2011 reinstated their salience. A transnational movement, whose dynamics still remain unclarified, raised the banner of republicanism and the response was swift as a burgeoning counter-revolution tried to tear it down. That was also true in what might be considered the American variant of what took place in the Middle East, namely, Occupy Wall Street. Thousands took to the streets in support of economic equality and against American counter-revolutionaries clustered in the Tea Party. Tolerance turned into a major problem as Islam became deified and the religious (and not so religious) right organized in Europe and the United States. No thinker is perhaps more salient when it comes to issues of tolerance, cosmopolitanism, and the liberal rule of law than Albert Camus, who won the Nobel Prize for Literature in 1956, and whose background left him poised between French and Algerian interests amid an anti-imperialist struggle in which terror was an acceptable tactic of both sides. In any event, liberal ideals were put to the test as millions of immigrants fled their homes and made their way to Europe in order to escape the deterioration of the Middle East in the aftermath of the Arab Spring and the reactionary responses to it. Cultures clashed, political conflicts flourished, and, often, provocations were made and terror was unleashed. How to defend tolerance under these conditions is a question with no easy answers. Nevertheless, the precondition for any answer is cultivating the cosmopolitan sensibility of religious and secular citizens alike.

1

Understanding Utopia

"Utopia" is perhaps the dirtiest word in the political lexicon. And there is some justification for that. The concept has often been employed to justify the worst totalitarian terror as well as otherworldly passivity in the face of real-life misery. Utopia conjures up images of demagogues, dreamers, fanatics, con artists, gullibility, apocalypse, and—perhaps above all—what Samuel Butler, the great Victorian satirist, called *erewhon* (or "nowhere" spelled backward). But this is only part of the story. Utopia has an anthropological appeal, especially for the wretched of the earth. Every civilization has its visions and views about paradise from which, given a certain cosmopolitan sensibility, other civilizations can learn. Utopia is never finished or, as Bertolt Brecht put it in his great play *Mahagonny* (1930), there is "always something missing." Memory often serves as the repository of forgotten hopes that are intertwined with visions of the *best life* and that contest the suffering produced by the slaughter-bench of history. This inherently incomplete and ill-defined concept of utopia has guided and inspired all the great mass movements of history and every genuine attempt to change the world for the better. Its traces appear in the most varied forms of art, philosophy, and religion. Often these utopian expressions conflict—and it is usually easier to get consensus on what constitutes dystopia than utopia. Nevertheless, utopian investigations can offer insights into what humanity might truly want—or not want—and thereby shape the image of the liberated society.

Envisioning utopia requires a bold imagination coupled with deep knowledge of humanity's cultural heritage. Utopian images have traditionally had a pastoral quality like the Garden of Eden, or the paradise once identified with the gardens of Persepolis (built by Cyrus the Great in the Persian city of Shiraz), "the land of milk and honey," or the heavenly gardens-for-the-rich in the film *Metropolis* (1927), or the world of leisure for the poor and the worker depicted in Jean Renoir's *A Day in the County*

(1946). All such visions rest on the longing for an organic society without alienation or reification, decadence, or the cultural and scientific complexity associated with modernity. Dystopian critics have condemned such utopias for ignoring the benefits of work, the enjoyment of politics, and the learning process that grows from failure. They have imagined the inhabitants of utopia as living in a quasi-drugged state, mindlessly happy, while lacking individuality and a sense of existential purpose. But such comfortable criticisms are easy to make by those who live comfortably. The wretched of the earth have always understood the liberating character of what Paul Lafargue (Marx's son-in-law) termed "the right to be lazy" and the utopian vision of a bountiful life marked by calm, health, leisure, joy, and play.

Utopia projects a world of social justice, economic equality, and radical democracy. But the "best life" is not reducible to the conquest of scarcity or institutional matters. Utopia projects a transformation with respect to how life is lived and the altered forms of behavior that privilege qualities like kindness and decency, charity and altruism, experimentation, and tolerance. It thereby provides a lens with which to view our world. The invocation of utopia makes us realize that what we have is not necessarily what we want and what we want is not necessarily all we can have. No system and no movement can ever fulfill the always untapped possibilities of human experience. Freedom and desire always outstrip the real. There will always be new possibilities for expanding the enjoyment of life and new discoveries of arbitrary constraint and repression. Few could conceive of the transgendered fifty years ago: the repression that was experienced and the courage to fight it.

Utopian ideals have traditionally had a complex and tension-ridden connection with reality. The way in which they are employed, in fact, provides deep insights into the character of radical political parties and social movements, their specificity, and how they operate. In his classic *Ideology and Utopia* (1936), Karl Mannheim noted how every genuine mass movement has been fueled by utopian impulses. Even social democracy had its visions of the best life crystallized in hugely popular works like Edward Bellamy's *Looking Backward* (1888). But such utopian ideals are always tainted and entangled with the particular interests and class base of the movement in question. A partial view of utopia is substituted for a vision consonant with its multiplicity and complexity—and its critical character gets lost. Utopia then turns into ideological slogans and forms suitable for mobilizing the masses. Only "free-floating intellectuals," according to Mannheim, can reflect upon this process and confront such ideological misrepresentations. To a certain extent, that is also true given the intellectual commitment that visualizing utopia requires. Unfortunately, Mannheim's position is usually criticized for justifying the intellectual's retreat from political life and as support for disengagement. Especially in periods of crisis and intense ideological conflict, however, it also serves as a plea for liberal politics and a rational stance with respect to what are often inherently emotional appeals.

Feelings of resentment and memories of exploitation by the exploited and disenfranchised render utopia susceptible to manipulation by authoritarian or totalitarian movements. Some have identified it with a racially pure or religiously homogeneous or ethnically cleansed society. Others have used it to justify their belief that a particular historical agent alone has the wisdom and knowledge to wield the avenging sword. This view informed the moral relativism of Lenin's vanguard party, its treatment of enemies from the standpoint of expediency, and later the purges of Stalin. The willingness to commit any crime in the name of utopian ends is the precondition of genocide and it contributed to what Camus considered the "pathology" of his age. Utopia is not a free pass by which the end is employed to justify any means that can bring it about. That is because the only way of justifying the end in question is by making reference to the means used in bringing it about. Calling on political actors to develop a plausible (not an absolute but a plausible!) relationship between ends and means is the first step in forming an emancipatory politics.

Human dignity constitutes both the means and the ends of utopia. Kant's famous injunction never to employ people as means to an end inherently confronts all attempts to manipulate utopia. It is always a matter of privileging the ability of individuals to explore their desires, expand their interests, and take control over their lives. So, for example, Marx and Engels never equated communism with any regime, not even the Paris Commune, but instead with the end of "pre-history" and the ideal of a world in which "the free development of each is the condition for the free development of all." In such a world, they believed, humanity can finally democratically determine its fate in common, consciously and without reference to external determinants like economic interest. Even more important, however, the classless society must serve as a society in which individualism will flourish.

Utopian experiments undertaken in the past cast a dark shadow over the seemingly pedestrian politics of the present. Many contemporary radicals remain enthralled by the image of that new society and the "new man" who would inhabit it. For many, utopia fuels slogans like "All Power to the Soviets!" and the "heroic stage" of the Russian Revolution (1918–1921) when it seemed that all things were possible: the cultural avant-garde working for the people, the abolition of money, the transformation of the nuclear family, the end of hierarchy, and international revolution intent upon creating regimes based on soviets or workers' councils. Trotsky crystallized this utopian communist outlook in his *Literature and Revolution* (1924) by insisting that ultimately: "Man will become immeasurably stronger, wiser, and subtler; his body will become more harmonized, his movements more rhythmic, his voice more musical. The forms of life will become dynamically dramatic. The average human type will rise to the heights of an Aristotle, a Goethe, or a Marx. And above this ridge new peaks will rise."

Nostalgia is a dangerous sentiment. It legitimately calls for recasting the past and understanding its value. But it can also easily obscure the arbitrary power exercised in those "heroic" years. The bloodshed, the confusion, the cruelty, and the poverty of those times vanish. Utopia was never real. An idealized perspective remains on what are today anachronistic institutions such as soviets in which, as it was once put to me, "everyone will control everything" (naturally without considering the number of meetings this would entail). Often what is identified with utopia is actually tainted by drab reality. That is why utopia involves a break with the real and, since every compromise involves accommodating alienation, the choice between all or nothing. Differences between existing parties and movements become negligible. Society turns into a seamless whole threatening all forms of critical reflection and individuality. The "system" becomes the problem, not any determinate set of institutions or policies, and anything reeking of reform is suspect. Nothing associated with real politics is radical enough and, in this way, the perfect becomes the enemy of the good. As an all or nothing proposition, therefore, utopian longings can justify passivity as easily as fanaticism. Either way, they are elemental ingredients in what Marx termed "the opium of the masses."

Utopia is inherently unfinished: the society or regime that views itself as utopian, or even firmly on the path to utopia, is dystopian by definition. That is because history does not move in linear fashion. Progress in one realm of society can occur while regression takes place in another. Extraordinary scientific breakthroughs, for example, often accompanied the rise of religious fundamentalism; cultural liberation flourished since the 1960s while economic equality increased. There is no uniform and prefabricated teleological process leading humanity to a happy end. Unresolved conflicts are often carried over from one epoch to the next. So, for example, racism and sexism and religious prejudices are pre-capitalist in character but play an important role in capitalist society—and, potentially beyond. Tensions exist not only between the whole and its dynamic parts but between the parts themselves. Micro-forms of violence and prejudice constantly appear and contradict self-satisfied notions of progress.

Calling for the mechanical translation of utopia into practice therefore misses the point; utopia celebrates the complexity and diversity of life, the different hopes of different cultures, and the multidimensional character of change. Only as a regulative ideal that might guide radical politics, but that resists being realized, can utopia highlight the inherent tension between humanity and its works, the power of the imagination and the demands of political power. Utopia will then provide radicals with both a sense of modesty by highlighting the ever-changing content and character of liberation. In order for that to occur, however, utopia must remain utopian. Only then can it illuminate the always limited exercise of freedom, and the ongoing need for at least the glimmer of an insight into the way forward.

2

The Enlightenment Lives!

Enlightenment thinking has traditionally been associated with progressive movements, as surely as the counter-enlightenment has been with those of a more reactionary sort. This has not always been the case but, historically, it has occurred with sufficient regularity to consider that claim as what John Dewey would have called a "warranted assertion." The Enlightenment and its cherished (if still unrealized) ideals of personal freedom were predicated on the liberal rule of law, an open society and what I have called the cosmopolitan sensibility.[1] Early political champions of this international intellectual movement of the seventeenth and eighteenth centuries targeted arbitrary exercises of institutional power, unearned privileges, religious intolerance, irrationalism, prejudice, and torture. These artificial impediments to liberty were seen as not only contributing to hatred and war but also to stunting the intellectual growth and psychological maturity of the individual.

With this in mind, "progress" gains a moral connotation and turns into a regulative ideal only insofar as it targets individual freedom. That institutions exist for providing or inhibiting opportunities available to individuals translates into a moral standpoint in which societies become subject to judgment in terms of the cultural and intellectual opportunities they offer their citizens. The "responsibility to protect" demanded of states by the United Nations is only the most rudimentary requirement. Economic equality and political liberty are less ends unto themselves than the necessary means for making life richer and new experiences possible. The "culture wars" of our time show that the defense of enlightenment values actually translates into a defense of the proposition that everyday people are capable of learning and, most crucially, learning about the other if given the right to do so. Exercising what is today called "difference" or identity is dependent on the institutional legitimacy accorded the liberal rule of law and civil rights as they developed during the great democratic revolutions of the eighteenth and nineteenth centuries.

Enlightenment political ideals are mostly Western, if not in their origin then in their institutional practice. They were embraced by liberal social movements, republican protests, and socialist labor movements concerned with political liberty and economic justice while committed to the scientific "disenchantment of the world"—and progress. It is certainly true that many great advocates of these ideals were anti-Semitic, racist, sexist, and bourgeois: Ben Franklin, Thomas Jefferson, Newton, Kant, Rousseau, or Voltaire. Others were less prejudiced: Spinoza, Montesquieu, Lessing, or Lichtenberg. None of them was totally ignorant of other cultures or an ivory tower intellectual shielded from public life. But, still, they tended to define the citizen, humanity, and the liberal rule of law in terms consonant with the interests of white male property-holders. In short, influenced by the prejudices of their time, they tended to identify the universal with the particular, and this misguided effort has become the source for most (post) modern criticisms of the Enlightenment. Its ideals of internationalism, the liberal state, and human rights have been used often enough to justify "great power politics," racist practices, and the exploitation of colonial and pre-capitalist territories. Nevertheless, the critical character and liberating insistence on individual autonomy associated with enlightenment thought and the liberal rule of law inherently contest the prejudices and exploitation of capitalism and imperialism with which the Enlightenment was originally intertwined.

Absolutism, dogmatism, and exploitation became the principle targets of the enlightenment legacy. That is still the case in the Western democracies and the Middle East. Its thinkers knew that humanity has many ways to pray, for example, and their primary political commitment was to the ideals of reciprocity and diversity. Religious institutions identifying their private interests with those of the public good thereby came under attack. The issue for most philosophes was not the abolition of religion but enabling the peaceful coexistence of multiple religions. In this way, Kant could carve out a place for religion "within the bounds of reason" and Voltaire could praise the country in which many religions flourished. Such religious relativism, however, probably insulted orthodox defenders of a faith even more than rank atheism that at least took their absolutist claims seriously. Herein lies the source, I think, of the contempt accorded liberalism and also democratic forms of socialism by the defenders of orthodoxy.

Enlightenment political thinking is irreducible to any specific agenda or fixed system of thought. It is best defined as a certain critical spirit with positive aims. As such, it impacted upon many institutions and their ideological outlooks including religion itself. Spinoza, Moses Mendelssohn, Lichtenberg became its advocates among Jews, still mostly stuck in provincial ghettoes, while concerns with natural rights and tempering dogma led many clergymen to break with their caste. The Abbe Sieyes who wrote "The Third Estate" (among the great revolutionary pamphlets of the French Revolution) is a case in point as are, later, those religious figures among the abolitionists and, still later, those who would play such an important role in the civil rights movement or, like the liberation theologians in Latin America, demand an end to authoritarian rule and the radical redistribution of wealth. This subterranean tendency seeking to realize enlightenment political values existed among Christians and Jews, and there is no reason to think that it is missing in Islam especially when considering those imams who supported the Arab Spring.

Looking at the matter through a slightly different lens, the pseudo-universalism propagated by many philosophes, which neglected women or people of color or the poor, came under attack most vehemently from social movements that highlighted the more robust critical and genuinely universal impulses of the Enlightenment. It became for them a matter of employing critique predicated on the universal claims underpinning the liberal rule of law against those who dismissed such concerns and identified with the discriminatory policies that basically privileged white men. Immanent criticism of the way in which universal claims and generalizable interests were denied became fundamental to the contestation of discriminatory laws by figures like Dr. Martin Luther King and Nelson Mandela. It was no different with the most progressive intellectuals representing republican and anti-imperialist movements in China, Iran, Latin America, and elsewhere.[2] Indeed, the same line of reasoning was strikingly apparent in the battle for a republic and the liberal rule of law during the Arab Spring.

Enlightenment political thinkers initially identified liberty with political rights such as freedom of religion and assembly, speech and ending arbitrary imprisonment. Only explicit legal prohibitions universally applied, they believed, should constrain individual action. Indeed, the logic of thinkers like John Locke or Adam Smith was transparent. The new liberal state should be kept weak so that "civil society" might be made strong. An "invisible hand" would regulate supply and demand and, ultimately, foster equality. Capitalism was seen as enhancing the public good as a "watchman state" by enabling individuals to compete and flourish. It was after all in civil society—the economy, the family, educational institutions, and the myriad associations of everyday life—that individuals became who and what they are.

But it soon became apparent that the "invisible hand" wasn't working: inequality was thriving, minorities were suffering from rank discrimination, and elites were unwilling to endanger their profits by attacking economic exploitation and oppressive economic conditions. If capitalist elites control investment, and working people and the poor constitute the majority, it makes sense that attacks on the welfare state should have usually been accompanied by broadsides targeting civil liberties and even the right to vote. Weakening liberal republican values became intertwined with the class conflict between workers seeking to maximize their wages and improve their daily lives as against capitalists wishing to maximize their profits and control their employees. Various experiments with tempering the whip of the market were undertaken in the first part of the twentieth century: social democrats demanded what today might be called "welfare rights," communists called for prioritizing "people over profits," workers' councils sought to fulfill the dream of participatory democracy with full economic equality, and, finally, postcolonial states attempted to follow their own economic course for communitarian social or religious purposes. These experiments mostly withered on the vine: social democracy lost its allure and its once revolutionary character, communism is utterly discredited, the workers' council has not kept pace with an increasingly complex globalized economy in theory or practice, and disillusionment reigns in the counter-revolutionary aftermath of the Arab Spring.

Enlightenment political thought is open to perversion like any other. Neo-conservative thinkers have used it to justify the "compassionate conservatism" of President George W. Bush.[3] Following 9/11, enlightenment values were employed to support an interventionist agenda in Afghanistan, Iraq, and elsewhere abroad while "color blind" arguments and legislation at home sought to perpetuate institutional racism and shrink the welfare state. Attacking the separation between church and state, no less than religious intolerance, was defended in terms of civil liberties; breaking international law was justified in terms of spreading human rights, anti-scientific attitudes by demands for pluralism; and the list could go on. The conservative manipulation of the enlightenment tradition was palpable in a general trend that rendered evidence irrelevant, as in the case of the "birthers" or the various justifications for invading Iraq and, more recently, opposing the nuclear treaty with Iran.

Much of the intellectual and radical post-1968 left tended toward versions of anarchism, communitarianism, often narrow identity politics, and post-structuralism. Enlightenment, science, reflection, and universals (though interestingly enough not "dialectics") tended to become dirty words. Their advocates stood accused of everything from supporting racism and sexism to helping bring about colonialism and virtually every catastrophe from the terror of the French Revolution to Stalin and Auschwitz.[4] The profound impact of the counter-enlightenment on authoritarian movements and its appeal to their pre-modern mass base was ignored. After all, no one any longer reads counter-enlightenment philosophers like Hamann or de Maistre or the majority of their colleagues.

And this only makes sense. Their bigotry, integral nationalism, religious dogmatism, celebration of tradition, subordination to authority, and reliance on intuition was far more radical than anything expressed by their enlightenment counterparts. Counter-enlightenment thinkers provide a worldview that is important for judging just how radical the philosophes were: so, for example, it takes some knowledge of forgotten academic painters of the time to understand just how remarkable the works are of van Gogh or Cézanne. Forgetting about distinctions between conflicting traditions of theory and practice leaves even the most perceptive critics wandering about in what Hegel termed "the night in which all cows are black." It betrays an unwillingness to acknowledge the connection between theory and practice as well as the material impact of ideas on movements. This combination offers some insight into why the Enlightenment's critical political heritage has been, if not exactly nullified, then taken for granted.

Terms like "republic," "rights," and "rule of law" are tossed about so regularly that they often seem bereft of meaning. Communist states called themselves republics and that remains the case with China, Iran, and North Korea; such states now interpret the "right" to national self-determination, yet another notion that arose amid the great bourgeois revolutions, as a justification for insulating their prejudices and authoritarianism from external criticism or international law. Elsewhere, enlightenment ideals of political liberty justify rollback of the welfare state and programs promoting economic equality and social justice. Not what constitutions say, which is always open to interpretations by conflicting interests, but enforcement of what Montesquieu termed "the spirit of the laws" is what marks the liberal republic and democracy in action.

Inhibiting the arbitrary exercise of institutional power (whether economic, political, or ideological) fueled the anti-communist revolutions of 1989 as well as the Arab Spring of 2011 and most other progressive movements of our age. The degree to which arbitrary institutional power is constrained ultimately determines just how "liberal" the liberal rule of law really is and whether social rights are actually in play. Little wonder that the modern counter-enlightenment is based in the political attempt to undermine the liberal rule of law and block the extension of social rights that are so important for exploited and disenfranchised minorities. In the aftermath of the Arab Spring, enlightenment political ideals have been thrown on the defensive once again. But then they never were ideologically hegemonic. The enlightenment spirit is still one of protest. It may have grown a bit rickety with age, but it is as emancipatory now as it was in earlier times. That is why the Enlightenment still provides such appeal for those who have struggled—and who are still struggling—for liberty in the first decades of the twenty-first century.

3

Rosa in Cairo

On May 1, 2012, I was in Cairo on a bright and sunny afternoon standing in Tahrir Square, the iconic spot symbolizing the Arab Spring, where thousands were celebrating the first anniversary of a tyrant's fall and the proclamation of a new liberal republic. I was part of a small delegation organized by US Academics for Peace and Conscience International. We were there to meet with representatives of various left-wing groups that were prominent in the Arab Spring and also bring some medicine into Gaza. The latter attempt did not turn out very well: we were stopped at the border. But we did meet activists and we learned much. As for me, I was inspired by what I saw in Tahrir Square, which also goes by the name of "Martyrs' Square": there were large placards baring the faces of different rebels who had made the ultimate sacrifice for democracy, there were bands and there were speeches, and there were any number of red flags and openly Marxist and socialist activists giving out educational materials and selling books and political buttons.

None of us had heard much reporting about concerns other than liberal ones, and it struck all of us how these socialist radicals had identified themselves with what had already become an international republican cause. Uprisings with similar goals and constituencies would constitute the Arab Spring—and they would have roughly the same enemies. The process began with the Green Revolution in Iran that was, admittedly, confused with respect to its reformist as against its institutionally radical transformative purpose. As with its successors, however, its supporters were urban, liberal, and culturally oriented toward the West. Later rebellions occurred with different degrees of success in Tunisia, Jordan, Algeria, Libya, Sudan, Yemen, and, of course, Egypt. All of them were spontaneous and rose from the ground up: it was almost as if the events of 2011 constituted a replay of 1989—only this time in the Middle East rather than the former Soviet Union.

Mainstream commentators, however, had as little meaningful to say about the dynamics of the former as about the latter. Transnational revolts generated by workers and everyday people left our political experts baffled. Their inability to provide an interpretive context, their narrow focus, their obsession with personal stories, and their reliance on the obvious had political implications. Conspiracy theories tended to fill the interpretive vacuum. In the United States, for example, Glenn Beck and his associates insisted that the Arab Spring was the result of nefarious radical sects working with (you've got to love it!) the American anti-authoritarian and feminist group Code Pink, which had been active in raising awareness about conditions in Gaza. Neo-conservatives added fuel to the fire. They keep wringing their hands over the new (alternately "existential" or "real") threats to Israel and the dangers of abandoning "reliable" long-time authoritarian allies of the United States. All their talk about spreading human rights in the Arab world, which served as among the justifications for invading Iraq, was suddenly forgotten. Real democracy didn't appeal to them: it apparently imperils our way of life.

Mainstream pundits were more reasonable. Interviews with everyday people were a must. Afterward there were the obligatory references to the role of "poverty"—as if poverty had not always gripped the masses of the Middle East and as if economic conditions had not been worse at other times. Then came the knowing remarks on bureaucratic corruption and the lack of democracy—as if corruption and dictators were recent inventions. For the yuppie and the technologically inclined, mention was also often made concerning the new organizing power of the Internet—as if there had never been a transnational uprising prior to the discovery of the computer. And that's that. All these factors are important in making sense of the Arab Spring but they provide no sense of historical specificity, radical tradition, or cosmopolitan impulses. Above all, they ignore the matter of political agency. The dynamics of what amazingly turned into a revolutionary chain reaction simply disappeared: it all became a media spectacle. Even progressives, it should be noted, evinced establishmentarian fixations above all with media, but also with leaders, elites, and conspiracy theory. No less than conservatives, for the most part, they showed a woeful ignorance of what Ernst Bloch termed "the underground history of the revolution."

Where then to look for an interpretive framework? Perhaps a good place to start is with Rosa Luxemburg (1871–1919). Early in my career I edited and translated *The Letters of Rosa Luxemburg* and published a short biography, *Rosa Luxemburg: A Revolutionary for Our Times*. Today her collected works are being edited by Peter Hudis and published in full by Verso Press; Jason Schulman has also edited an important debate over her salience, *Rosa Luxemburg: Her Life and Legacy* (Palgrave). Margarethe von Trotta directed a movie about her life, masses still gather in Berlin to commemorate the day of her death, and her name has been used for the research institute of the Left Party in Germany. In short, sources are available, but Rosa (like so many other figures in the socialist and Marxist traditions) remains almost unknown to mainstream political science in America.

Everyone called her Rosa. A libertarian socialist of exceptional charisma and charm, a powerful intellectual and a genuine celebrity in the international labor movement, Luxemburg was brutally murdered by proto-Nazi thugs in 1919 at the age of forty-eight. A Marxist of the old school, Rosa would surely have been thrilled by what transpired in the Middle East and probably also by the anti-communist revolutions of 1989. There was nothing special about her commitment to republicanism and social equality. What made her unique was the special emphasis she placed upon the role of democratic consciousness, internationalism, and what I would call a cosmopolitan pedagogy whereby one exploited community learns from another in an ongoing revolutionary process.

All this played a crucial role in the rebellions that cascaded from one nation to another in the Middle East. Luxemburg's *Mass Strike, Party, and Trade Unions* (1906) explored this dynamic. Her pamphlet was inspired by a series of spontaneous protests that began in Baku in 1902, spread to Kiev and St. Petersburg, and ultimately engulfed the entire Russian Empire in 1905. The first parliament in Russian history resulted from strikes whose spontaneity tended to obscure the years of underground work by unionists and political activists. Luxemburg saw in the mass strike a justification for privileging the institutional aims of the socialist movement as well as the untapped democratic capacities of the disenfranchised and the exploited. In her world, dominated by authoritarian regimes like so much of the Middle East, this meant—above all—highlighting the prospect of a republic. The mass strike would first express itself locally in the towns and cities through the actions of workers and then spread to the countryside; bourgeois liberal aims would unify the masses with liberal elements of the elite and, ultimately, bring about regime change; afterward, of course, new political and economic class conflicts would arise over questions of governmental structure, leadership, and policy. Does this sound familiar?

Luxemburg maintained that the mass strike crystallized decades of mostly unacknowledged subterranean activism. She was a brilliant economist who (perhaps mistakenly) believed in the inevitable breakdown of capitalism. In any event, however, economic deprivation served her only as the backdrop for political action. Crucial were less the "objective" circumstances, or the crisis, than the radical consciousness ready to make use of it. Luxemburg knew her history. She embraced an explicitly political tradition of international revolt that reached back over 1905 to 1848 and to the century of democratic revolution that extended from 1688 to 1789. Other traditions also come to mind. The international assault on communism in 1989 harks back to the birth of Solidarity in Poland in 1980, the Prague Spring of 1968, the Hungarian Revolt of 1956, and the Berlin uprising of workers in 1953. The Arab Spring is not simply some exotic set of unique events, but rather has a place in this great tradition. The Carnegie Endowment for International Peace noted in February of 2010 that more than three thousand labor protests had taken place in Egypt since 2004. Those brave rebels demonstrating in the streets of Cairo surely reflected upon them as well as the Green Revolution in Iran, and the other uprisings in neighboring countries, as they chanted: "Tunisia is the solution!"

Written amid the factory takeovers in Warsaw during 1905, Luxemburg's letters show her enthusiasm for the dramatic attempts to introduce democracy into everyday life as well the burgeoning "soviet" or "council" movement. Her primary concern was with proletarian mobilization and introducing a participatory form of economic democracy. But she never abandoned the republican goals of the mass strike. Only a republic, she knew, could secure civil liberties. Luxemburg never equated democracy with the will of the majority or even social justice; she knew that, perhaps above all, democracy rested on the protection of the minority. Her famous line from *The Russian Revolution* (1918) still rings true: "Freedom is always and exclusively freedom for the one who thinks differently." Luxemburg anticipated that the communist suppression of bourgeois democracy in 1917 would unleash a dynamic of terror. She also recognized that the exercise of terror is, ultimately, a sign of weakness—not strength. This same knowledge surely informed those rebels in the streets of Cairo and elsewhere in the Middle East; it probably informs the thinking of the new counter-revolutionary authoritarians in the Middle East as well.

Max Weber famously noted that the viability of any state rests on common recognition of its legitimate monopoly over the means of coercion. The mosque and the military thus remain the pivots of power: their choices set the stage for what is possible. The mosque defines everyday morality, challenges globalizing impulses, and controls paramilitary organizations. As for the military, it is often the employer of last resort, the self understood defender of state sovereignty, and national identity, whose elite status is taken for granted. Both the mosque and the military threaten the expanded freedoms associated with cosmopolitanism, individualism, and, of course, the liberal rule of law. What Stendhal termed the red and the black, the military and the church/mosque, have been the pillars of counter-enlightenment and counter-revolutionary politics since 1789. Such was the case in Europe and it is also the case in the Middle East. Insurgents during the Arab Spring were successful insofar as they were able to keep counter-revolutionary interests from acting as autonomous agents in political affairs.

Revolution is a daunting task, but running a country the day after is even more daunting. New liberal republics in economically disadvantaged circumstances had to navigate a swirl of conflicting economic interests and illiberal institutional claims. Soon enough storms were darkening the Arab Spring. Revolutions in Tunisia, Jordan, Egypt, and elsewhere fell into disarray as activists attempted to translate democratic ideals into institutional reality. The Arab Spring transgressed national borders, challenged unique notions of identity, and exploded not only popular belief in a "clash of civilizations" but the sometimes explicit and sometimes implicit racism behind claims that Arabs are unwilling and unable to identify with liberal principles. The Arab Spring was marked by spontaneous revolts, lack of charismatic leaders, youthful exuberance, and disdain for more traditional forms of organizational discipline. That is what made these revolutions so appealing.

Established monarchies trembled in Bahrain and even in Saudi Arabia. And for good reason: their authoritarian state structures were marked by arbitrary exercises of power, labyrinthine forms of hierarchy, corruption, and rank cronyism. Lack of civil liberties, fairness, transparency, and institutional accountability were—along with lack of economic opportunity—perhaps the primary sources of revolt for the partisans of the Arab Spring during the Arab Spring. They all crystallized in the idea of a liberal republic. So it was that King Abdullah II of Jordan acceded to demands for a more fairly elected parliament and democratic elections took place in various states and, most successfully, in Tunisia. Always there were institutional obstacles to confront. Speaking truth to power proved insufficient. The Arab Spring floundered on its inability to deal with internal weakness and conflicts, disorganization and sectarianism, but its lack of success ultimately derived from its inability to deal with the stalwarts of counter-revolution.

Rosa never guaranteed success, and the mass strike is not some reproducible blueprint for the future. It also does not provide a full explanation of the Arab Spring. Empirical factors come into play and more than a century separates the Russian mass strike from what transpired in the Middle East. But Luxemburg's theory of the mass strike at least provides the beginnings of an interpretive framework. This extraordinary intellectual activist—too much the revolutionary for socialist reformers and too much the democrat for communist revolutionaries—still has much to teach about international solidarity, radical democracy, and a meaningful notion of class politics. Her thinking provides links with the past, insights into the present, and inspiration for the future. Rosa may not have the final word on the great events of our time: but especially her cosmopolitan internationalism gives us a place to start in making sense of them.

4

Counter-Revolution, Enlightenment, Republic

A Cosmopolitan Sketch

Counter-revolution and revolution are concepts that derive from eighteenth-century and nineteenth-century Europe. They were generated by bourgeois-democratic rebellions that spread from England in 1688 and the United States in 1776 to France, the Netherlands, and elsewhere beyond Europe. The counter-revolutionary responses were swift and forthcoming. Events were different in different nations just as the Enlightenment and conservative reactions were different in Scotland than in France or Germany. Empirical obsessions usually obscure the larger picture. More than that, however, they elide the crucial question about whether this complex of enlightenment, republic, and counter-revolution is confined to Europe. This is important given the pressing need to understand the transnational Arab Spring of 2011 and the transnational counter-revolution it inspired. No less than with the anti-communist revolutions in Eastern Europe of 1989, mainstream commentators have been unable to provide any meaningful structural analysis of events in the Middle East. Perhaps that is because (whether out of prejudice or ignorance or both) they refuse to situate the Arab Spring in the tradition of other transnational bourgeois revolutions that occurred in Western and Eastern Europe. Of course, in turn, this can only reinforce beliefs in the rigid division divide between "civilizations" that has created so much misunderstanding. Indeed, the lack of structural inquiry contributes to the existing provincialism of the social sciences—both in the Occident and the Orient.

The Arab Spring was inspired by the cosmopolitan liberal ideals of times past. It too was an international revolt of primarily urban workers, bourgeois, and intellectuals against similar authoritarian regimes buttressed by the traditional stalwarts of European reaction: the military and religious institutions or, in this case, the mosque. How the rebellions fared depended largely upon the ideological and organizational unity of the movement and the response of its traditional enemies. Cosmopolitanism, individual freedom, reciprocity of rights and duties, and reliance on the liberal rule of law contest the core values of traditionalism and/or authoritarian rule. Two mutually exclusive political standpoints thus emerged that were animated less by an explicit dogma or agenda than an ethos—that social action can either strengthen or weaken.

Intent upon eliminating stubborn prejudices and traditional hierarchies, and realizing what were roughly enlightenment political ideals associated with liberty, the bourgeois revolutions shared a common spirit, sense of purpose, and opposition from similar counter-revolutionary forces. Urban classes with an interest in furthering science, education, technology, and the secular state everywhere engaged in attempts to disenchant the world. Everywhere they squared off against provincial dogmatists and xenophobes who insisted that democracy was a foreign import, tradition was sacrosanct, and an inherent hatred existed between "us and them." The situation is roughly the same in the Middle East where the military considers itself sovereign, patriarchal and pre-modern traditions are embraced because they seemingly always existed, and religious hatreds between Sunni and Shia have burst into the open. Such were the circumstances in which partisans of the Arab Spring made their pitch for a secular republic while the beneficiaries of primarily religious, tribal, and military institutions frantically attempted to preserve their authority.

"Restoration" was the term given to the autocratic regimes that followed the end of democratic revolutions and then the Napoleonic Wars. It was a fitting designation applicable in one way or another to every counter-revolution. Its aim has always been to "restore" elements of some "golden age" in which elite privileges of this or that class or gender or ethnicity were taken for granted. That the "good old days" were never quite that good is irrelevant. Justification was required to counter the democratic and egalitarian claims by disenfranchised and exploited classes and groups. In theory and practice, the transnational Restoration of 1815–1848 following Napoleon's defeat advocated a return to monarchy, aristocratic hierarchies, and religious ritual. Its partisans fought modernity by opposing universal claims with integral nationalism, rights with communitarian mores, reason with faith, discourse with intuition, and democracy with inherited authority. It's not difficult to imagine what would have been their later reactions to the new demands for social equality and ethical reciprocity raised by the "other"—women, people of color, young people without rights, those without property, the "alien" and the foreigner.

Intolerance for the other became enmeshed with religious principles and counter-revolutionary interests. So, for example, Wahhabi extremists in Saudi Arabia and the reactionary revolutionary guards in Iran both defend the Sunni or Shia vision of the "real" Islam through narratives privileging behavior associated with the traditional and pre-modern social order. Their sectarian employment of Islam is reinforced by integral nationalism, and rigidly provincial understandings of national culture, against cosmopolitan forms of "tolerance." That is because liberal understandings of civil liberties are seen by fanatics on both sides of the religious divide as making blasphemy acceptable while resting on "abstract" universal notions of justice and law that appeal only to "rootless cosmopolitans," ivory-tower "intellectuals," and the "Other."

Counter-revolutionary thinking grounds identity in traditions with organic roots and the support of elites who justify their power by reference to custom or God. Incapable of grasping why the (supposedly happy) subaltern turned against the hegemonic religious culture, counter-revolutionaries tend to invoke conspiracies that range from the *Protocols of Zion* to more recent convictions that Israel and the United States colluded in the attack on the World Trade Center of 9/11 and, after initially provoking the Arab Spring to destabilize the region, were "really" behind the authoritarian misadventures of those religious and military groups that sought to crush it.

Such beliefs did not come out of nowhere. A brilliant novel like *The Prague Cemetery* (2010) by Umberto Eco shows how conspiratorial theory and practice have been traditional pillars of the counter-revolution. What I have termed "conspiracy fetishism" has no use for rational discourse, normal evidentiary standards, empirical justification, provisional truths, or falsifiability. Conspiracy fetishism is inherently self-referential and it is based on intolerance and dogmatic faith. The attitudinal ethos underpinning it thus fits perfectly with the counter-revolutionary contempt for tolerance, rights, reason, and the liberal rule of law. It also fits with the sort of integral nationalism that has always intoxicated the counter-revolution. Tensions between the enlightenment and counter-enlightenment political worldviews would simmer in Europe throughout the next two centuries and in 2011 first in Tunisia and then throughout the Middle East.

Were the Arab Spring and the counter-revolutionary responses to it *sui generis* or not? Providing a meaningful answer depends upon moving beyond the lazy truism that events in different circumstances are different. There are striking similarities between the Arab Spring and the nineteenth-century liberal democratic revolutions in Europe as well as the counter-revolutions that followed. Highlighting the general dynamics not only helps us better understand what transpired but also projects a more cosmopolitan and less ethnocentric sense of history and politics. Approaching the mater in this way rejects the assumption that republicanism is the exclusive domain of any particular culture or region. Indeed, making this historically and politically clear offers material backing for claims that Islamic nations are not simply bereft of democratic ideals and longings.

Where do the similarities lie? In 2010–2011, a transnational revolutionary wave gripped the Middle East. The spontaneous uprisings were foreshadowed by ongoing yet generally unreported political activity: Egypt alone witnessed more than three thousand protests in the years preceding the Arab Spring. The kind of mass strike envisioned by Rosa Luxemburg was operative. The Green Revolution in Iran targeted the religious authoritarianism instituted by Khomeini's Islamic Revolution of 1979. The uprising spread to Lebanon in 2005 and then to Tunisia, Syria, Egypt, Yemen, and Libya before circling back to Lebanon and the "You Stink" revolts of 2015. Grounded in the cities, all these uprisings were supported by intellectuals, young people without job prospects, unemployed technocrats, nascent bourgeois, and workers. No less than in Western democratic revolutionary movements of the nineteenth and twentieth centuries, the mass base for the Arab Spring was the cluster of urban classes and strata whose identities and material hopes were entangled with globalization and modernity.

The Arab Spring was an extraordinary drama that played throughout the Middle East. Movements in different nations built upon one another because their mass base was similar and their political agents shared the same cultural and political goals. All of them wished to eliminate religious constraints (such as the Iranian "morality police") while expanding the range of available life choices and experiences. They also realized that the practice of diversity and individuality requires commitment to the liberal rule of law, civil rights, and the assault upon those authorities and institutions that attempted to constrict their exercise. No less than in the West, therefore, Middle Eastern activists envisioned new republics or, in Iran, a radical political reform of the existing republic. There were few actual parties involved in the Arab Spring and little talk about institutions or policies other than parliament and sometimes an independent judiciary.

Counter-revolutionaries throughout the Middle East were correct in maintaining that the rebels had little use for the traditionalism of agrarian society and village life. As for the military and the mosque, initially they were little more than lukewarm defenders of the Arab Spring and what Machiavelli would have called its "unarmed prophets." To be sure, dictators like Assad and Saddam and Gaddafi were never advocates of liberal political principles. But they did consider themselves secular "modernizers" opposed to the superstitions and practices of traditionalism. They also were not usually heirs of aristocratic families as were so many higher-ranking officers of the European and Russian counter-revolutions. As for Islam, it often expressed something radical and emancipating by confronting the religious beliefs of Western imperialists and, just as with the anti-communist Catholic Church in Eastern Europe, defending anti-imperialism and even secular rebels. In most of the Middle East, however, Islamic muftis were employees of the state. Appointed and with their fatwas approved by dictators, their interests often paralleled those of the state and they tended to provide ideological legitimation for secular institutions and agendas. But there is a sense in which this was always a marriage of convenience. The Arab Spring threatened both the military and the mosque and thus, unsurprisingly, the enemy of an enemy often became a friend—at least for so long as circumstances dictated.

Counter-revolution is reactionary in a literal sense: it reacts to events and its particular character is defined by what it opposes. But there are different degrees of opposition as there are different degrees of authoritarian rule. ISIS and similar expressions of Islamic extremism provide the ultimate standard. They react against cultural individualism and especially gender liberation with inherited tribal and patriarchal values: the Western ethical-legal framework with an "originalist" reading of Sharia law, the Western bureaucratic state with visions of a caliphate; Western understandings of "humanity" with an intensified distinction between friend and enemy or, better, the righteous and the infidel; and Western ideals of progress with the exaltation of the feudal, and the disenchantment of the world with its reenchantment as a product of God. The austerity and asceticism associated with ISIS, al-Qaeda, and the Taliban also appear as pious reactions to the hedonism and commercialism associated with globalization. All of them speak primarily to those who are poverty stricken—and recognize that this is their fate. Ernst Bloch noted in *Heritage of Our Times* (1935) that "man does not live by bread alone, especially when he doesn't have any." In any event, ISIS and other organizations of Islamic extremists turn economic underdevelopment into a virtue and, in doing so, offer an overarching alternative to the totality of Western society.

Their leaders should be thought of as what Meera Nanda termed "prophets looking backward." All of them privilege authority over liberty, unquestioning faith over critical reflection, and the community over the individual. All of them have their problems with the rights of women and gays, abortion and patriarchy, censorship and democracy. Each rejects the separation of church and state and the critique of patriarchal hierarchies. Each insists upon the legitimacy of traditions simply because they exist. Intolerance and dogmatism are built into this mode of thinking if only because (as with other religions) discussion is limited by the holy words of an inerrant Bible, an infallible Pope, Islamic Sharia, or the Jewish *Halakha*. The absolutist or the true believer is still engaged in a battle over whether a single religion (or a single interpretation of that religion) should dominate public life. This is not simply a matter of the church, the synagogue, and the mosque acting in accordance with divine law against the profane (although it can be turned into that) but of ideological primacy and institutional self-preservation. Thus, the more dramatic the demand for reciprocity, the more fundamental is the response.

Yet it was not the religious hatred between Sunni and Shia that sparked the bloody political conflicts of the Middle East in the twenty-first century; it was the other way around. These two branches of Islam had lived more or less peacefully for generations. But that changed dramatically with the invasion of Iran by Iraq (over imperialist ambitions and unsettled colonial borders) and then with the American invasion of Iraq in 2003 by the Bush administration. A chain reaction of events produced the erosion of sovereignty in Afghanistan, Iraq, Lebanon, Libya, Syria, and Yemen: millions were killed, wounded, or driven into exile; the environmental damage was almost unimaginable; fear and hatred of the West spread beyond what had originally been the small international terrorist organization known as al-Qaeda; proxy wars flourished with any number of sponsors and paramilitary organizations; and ideological disorientation ran deep. Conspiracies and phobias mingled and fueled new feelings of integral nationalism, radical forms of religious identity, and old prejudices.

All of this has parallels in the counter-revolutions waged against the European bourgeois revolutions extending from the late seventeenth into the twentieth centuries. That is particularly true of the ideological mindset. Heightening the differences and hatreds between "us and them" assumed crucial political importance in shaping reactionary political worldviews. Counter-revolutionaries of the early nineteenth century had already ideologically juxtaposed the concepts of *civilization* (rational, light, and cultivated) and *Kultur* (instinctual, deep, and organic), for example, long before France and Germany manipulated them to justify their integral nationalism and imperialist ambitions in World War I. Cultural provincialism champions the "good old days" and feelings of belonging while intolerance politically reinforces both.

Fundamentalism in the Middle East should be seen in the same counter-revolutionary light. It fuels traditional anti-imperialist resentments against the West as well as imperialist ambitions of its own while offering visions of a golden age as an alternative to the bureaucratic, corrupt, and ruthless "modernizing state" run by Arab dictators. Islamic fundamentalism considers the Koran capable of answering every problem, just as Christian and Jewish fundamentalists view their Bibles, and it is the work of the righteous to create the appropriate conditions in which the old laws can be followed. Thus, tensions existed between the military and the mosque in spite of their shared suspicions of the Arab Spring.

A word is necessary about the Muslim Brotherhood. Though begun in Egypt in 1928, it has branches in many nations and serves as a political party that tries to fill the void when the mosque is hijacked by the state. Some of these parties are pragmatic and others dogmatic and their character becomes clear when confronting the options facing them. In Tunisia, for example, rebels led by the labor unions produced a post-revolutionary coalition of liberal parties and interests that capitalized on the military remaining neutral as they battled the institutional and ideological power of the mosque. That Tunisia proved the most successful democratic experiment of the Arab Spring is no accident; it was predicated on a military disaffected from the old regime, and thus amenable to the new one, and a Tunisian Islamic movement willing to surrender power after it had become clear that majority support was lacking. That democracy remains imperiled in Tunisia does not invalidate the original experiment or hopes for the future.

In Egypt, by contrast, the relationship between the military and the mosque is somewhat more dramatic and complex since the mufti of the official Sunni mosque (or the al-Azhar) is appointed by the sovereign while the Muslim Brotherhood is a relatively autonomous organized political movement that allows Muslims to confront what they consider a secular mosque and a secular state. Little wonder that the Egyptian Brotherhood should have been subject to harsh repression especially under the presidential dictatorship of Gamal Abdel Nasser and now under President Abdel Fattah el-Sisi basically with the blessings of the Azhar. Thus, while uprisings in Tahrir Square pitted republican rebels against President Hosni Mubarak's military, the Muslim Brotherhood in Egypt acted very differently than its Lebanese or Tunisian counterpart: it initially stood on the sidelines and entered the fray only after Mubarak had fallen and republican institutions had already been proclaimed.

With mounting economic problems, and democratic forces incapable of surmounting its disorganized and fractious character, the Muslim Brotherhood dominated the first parliamentary elections. Ultimately, it didn't matter. The military waited patiently. And it was right to do so. On assuming power, the Brotherhood and its president, Mohamed Morsi, immediately began acting capriciously and autocratically with regard to other parties and religious minorities. Civil liberties were often suspended in dealing with dissidents and the secular rebels of the Arab Spring, while military leaders and political officials connected with the old regime (including an aging Mubarak and his sons) were incarcerated—or worse. In short, the Muslim Brotherhood had not internalized the democratic ethos. Disillusionment soon reached the point where Al-Nour, a (fundamentalist) Salafi party previously allied with the Brotherhood, supported the military in overthrowing President Morsi. The Muslim Brotherhood had no plan to deal with the workers in the largest business in Egypt, namely, the military, or the effects of diminishing tourism. Egypt found itself in an economic crisis, the sovereign remained in doubt, new institutions lacked political legitimacy, and anti-democratic measures were masked by religious justifications.

When the military finally intervened, it did so with ruthless efficiency. Insisting that the country was being saved from chaos, which has been a traditional justification for military intervention in the political process, its generals jailed leaders of the Muslim Brotherhood, banned demonstrations, and (again) curtailed civil liberties. The prisons were soon overflowing: more than ten thousand people were detained, two thousand shot, and the Egyptian branch of the Muslim Brotherhood disbanded. Already compromised after the first election, and its manipulation by then-president Morsi of the Brotherhood, the new judiciary lost its independence. Mubarak, his sons, and his cronies were freed from jail and all indictments against them for corruption, murder, and torture were quashed. The Muslim Brotherhood was driven underground and, in desperation, surrendered its traditional pacifism, took up arms in halfhearted fashion, and promptly found itself labeled a "terrorist" organization. But it was not the Muslim Brotherhood alone that sacrificed principle to exigency. Many liberal activists initially applauded the military attack on Islam. They soon found Egypt succumbing to the "restoration" of precisely the kind of authoritarian state that they had previously rebelled against. Hegel would have called this this the "cunning" of history.

Peaceful protests in Syria, meanwhile, called upon President Bashar al-Assad to introduce the kind of multiparty elections he had promised many times over the years as a substitute for decades of governing under emergency decree. The response was brutal and, quickly enough, Assad's military attempted to crush the nascent democratic movement whose base was, as usual, in the cities. Important for present purposes is that there was no Muslim Brotherhood and, as the rebellion turned violent, its dozens of political parties and interests made way for the most ideological and internally disciplined among them, namely, al-Qaeda and al-Nusra. Not only did this undermine the initially liberal democratic and secular character of the rebellion, but it also identified it, or the most organized and religious parts of it, with counter-revolutionary terror.

Tensions between Sunnis and Shia exploded and, with the military on both sides exhausting each other like two aged boxers, the path was paved for foreign intervention by other counter-revolutionary forces; Saudi Arabia intervened on the side of the mostly Sunni rebels as did ISIS while Iran and Russia, which entered the conflict in 2015, provided military support for Assad and his Alawite branch of Shia. ISIS and the worst among the rebels, al-Qaeda and the al-Nusra Front, now control nearly two-thirds of the country; Assad still controls most of the rest and, notably, the democratic elements of the original rebellion have vanished. Syria has witnessed the most terrible triumph of the counter-revolution.

Yet it remains difficult simply to accept the old platitude that "the more things change, the more they remain the same." Things did change with the Arab Spring just as they changed in Europe following the age of bourgeois revolution and the events of 1848. The new parliaments that arose in so many Middle Eastern nations were mostly emasculated. They were as ineffectual as the leftovers from 1848 during the Second Empire of Napoleon III and the rule of Bismarck. As in Europe, however, parliament became an established institution with new legitimacy among the (particularly urban) citizenry. Elections began being held regularly, even in Egypt (2015), as the conflict became palpable between defenders of parliamentary democracy and those intent upon weakening its powers while strengthening their own. The conflict was actually over sovereignty and, consequently, the liberal republic became a rallying cry for the new agents of change: secular intellectuals, disillusioned youth, alienated professionals, cosmopolitan bourgeois, unions and workers.

This was roughly the same mass base as what drove the European republican events of 1848, the uprisings in the aftermath of uprisings of World War I, and the anti-communist revolutions of 1989 in our own time. All were transnational, and they all shared ideological commitments to liberal republican values. A new cosmopolitan sensibility, and a new form of international solidarity. It was no different with the counter-revolutions fueled by the military and the church/mosque, non-urban actors, and beneficiaries of the old order: its defenders remain as authoritarian, close-minded, and provincial as ever. They still have little use for the liberal understanding of progress, complexity and diversity, science and the disenchantment of the world, and—of course—an expanded world of individual opportunity and the pursuit of new knowledge. The desires of progressive people in the Occident and the Orient are not so very different. If nothing else, the Arab Spring liberated the dynamics of (conservative and liberal) politics from provincial confines and turned the radical enterprise into a cosmopolitan project. And the story is still unfolding.

5

Tolerating Intolerance

Confusion grows daily
Oh, holy Koran! Oh, eternal calm!

—Goethe, *West-Ostlicher Divan*

Whatever crushes individuality is despotism, by whatever name it may be called and whether it professes to be enforcing the will of God or the injunctions of men.

—John Stuart Mill, *On Liberty*

An old friend once told me that being a decent person means having a guilty conscience. And there was enough to feel guilty about as 2015 unfolded. Ethical uncertainty over how a liberal society should deal with the intolerant has become strikingly evident following the murders of four French Jews in a kosher grocery and twelve editors and staff members of *Charlie Hebdo*, a satirical magazine located in Paris, by partisans of al-Qaeda and, its rival, ISIS. Fear of blaming the victim and perhaps providing support to Israel has led some very decent people to minimize a burgeoning European anti-Semitism and the allure of Islamic fanaticism. Given the terror and bloodshed produced throughout the region by Israel and the United States, many are concerned about the use of a double standard in discussing terrorism. Also, if satirizing Mohammed the Prophet is permitted, it is difficult to understand why the same behavior is deemed criminal when applied to the Holocaust. *Charlie Hebdo* may have been critical of religion as such, yet its staff targeted Islam more frequently than other faiths. They did not take the possibly dire consequences of their blasphemous provocations seriously enough. Instead they blithely assumed the universal "right" to free speech that, in fact, many states deny in principle and even liberal states never fully translate into practice. Only an assault on the double standard coupled with an invigorated cosmopolitan sensibility can turn back the rising tide of intolerance.

But fanatics of whatever cause revel in the double standard—especially when it benefits them. They adamantly reject reciprocity under the liberal rule of law or anything remotely resembling a cosmopolitan sensibility. So far as they are concerned, reciprocity is for the "Other" and it has no role to play in their world. Everything is always about them and their beliefs: looking at any other stance is superfluous. Fanaticism can be understood as an exaggerated narcissism fueled by rage, contemptuous of discourse, and always ready for violence (discursive or physical) against the "Other." It is not a matter of either permitting or prohibiting satire or criticism of both the Prophet and the Holocaust. So far as the fanatic is concerned, he should be able to criticize what he likes while censoring what he wishes. Whether it is an Orthodox Jew gunning down Arabs in a mosque, or Islamic extremists blowing up a discotheque, the fanatic always provides an objective apology, as communists used to call it, for existing stereotypes. That is not a by-product of extremism but rather a deeply embedded part of its purpose, namely, to intensify the distinction between friend and foe. To this extent it also makes sense that fanatics will turn on more moderate coreligionists; Israeli Prime Minister Rabin was assassinated by an Orthodox Jew in 1995, for example, and it makes sense that ISIS has slaughtered other Muslims, humiliated their women, and sold them into slavery. In short, abolishing the double standard requires not only an ethical commitment in the abstract but also one that challenges conventional loyalties.

Armchair politicos like to claim that public actions by those who protested the murders in the offices of *Charlie Hebdo* are nothing more than spectacles that don't deal with the "real" issues. But then participating in public protest and investigating the real issues are not mutually exclusive endeavors. Public action has often enough generated support for policies and turned symbols into issues. That is especially true in France where any political person remembers the huge mass demonstrations of July 14, 1936, that inaugurated the anti-fascist Popular Front. Critics of "Je Suis Charlie" were notably remiss in suggesting alternative ways for citizens to express their grief and solidarity with the victims. Some suggested that "Je Suis Charlie" was a mask for anti-Islamic and anti-Arab sentiments. Yet the organizers explicitly excluded anti-immigrant and neo-fascist parties from participating, made fervent pleas for the protection of civil liberties, and championed solidarity among diverse religious and political leaders as well as everyday citizens. New calls were subsequently heard for targeted employment and educational programs and better integration of Arabs into civil society.

The masses fought long and hard for the right to free speech and public assembly: No less than white Europeans, Arabs and Muslims want and deserve to be heard. But historical experience teaches that their hopes for a better future rest upon modern states in which they can exercise their civil liberties rather than medieval caliphates ruled by emirs according to arbitrary interpretations of Sharia law that condemn art, music, free expression, and non-Koranic education. Religious institutions have always tended to treat free speech as a danger to public morals and an affront to the faith. Whether *Charlie*'s cartoons were in bad taste, or whether the magazine satirized the mosque more than the church, is irrelevant. Freedom of speech involves testing limits and *Charlie* had the right to choose its targets without asking permission. In a liberal society, writers and artists are not required to be "even-handed" let alone produce what a specific audience wants to read or view. Its editors were also entitled to expect peaceful criticisms of their views.

Freedom of speech has always harbored the danger of blasphemy and, by its very nature, threatens fixed beliefs and rigid dogmas. Most states still deny their citizens that right which, according to Enlightenment thinkers from Kant to Hannah Arendt, is the foundation for *all* other political rights.[1] It underpins the right to assembly, religion, and the political action necessary for making the public good transparent and confronting the arbitrary use of institutional power. Or, to put it another way, free speech makes it possible for the public to think. Private institutions like the church, the synagogue, and the mosque should in principle have as much (or little) say in determining public priorities than the chamber of commerce or some union. The extent to which they do is the extent to which tyranny reigns. Worse: it is the extent to which intolerance is turned into a virtue.

Tolerance implies neither passivity nor relativism. An opinion offensive to one group can—and should—be confronted by another. Those intent on repressing free speech are not only intellectually lazy but, also, cowardly. By the same token, however, free speech is not a free pass: writers and media pundits should assume responsibility for what they say rather than cower behind the First Amendment. Calls for repressing opposing views express weakness rather than strength. Indeed, Rosa Luxemburg insisted in her great pamphlet *The Russian Revolution* (1918) that freedom only for the members of a ruling party or church is actually no freedom at all: "Freedom is always and exclusively freedom for the one who thinks differently."

Looking to the community to protect free speech for the minority has always been a questionable strategy: there is no reason for the subaltern to trust the hegemon. The issue in a democracy is not simply a matter of ensuring the will of the majority but, perhaps more importantly, protecting the rights of the minority. The condemnation of Socrates shows the importance of defending the public space in which minorities not only participate but should be encouraged to do so. Political rights are meaningless without social responsibility: Cultural and religious intolerance are today being generated not by those who criticize the constraints of liberal society but rather those who deny its freedoms tout court. Thomas Mann liked to say that there is never too much intelligence in the world.[2] And there is never too much freedom either. Tolerating intolerance presents both a threat and a challenge: navigating the two successfully is the precondition for securing the future of liberal society.

6

Albert Camus

On the Fiftieth Anniversary of His Death

Albert Camus was a man of France and Algeria who, like every great writer, touches the young. Camus spoke to the generation that came of age in the 1940s and 1950s—amid the Cold War and as the Algerian Revolution was ripping France apart. But he was also the most popular writer among the students of the 1960s. I first read Camus as a teenager and I remember applauding his humanism, his strange mixture of pessimism and optimism, and his ability to engage himself in the political world without forgetting about the desire for personal happiness. Even today, nearly every high school student is introduced to one or another of his works. And that only makes sense: he was a provocative novelist who dealt with the perennial concerns of philosophy. He was a man of the Mediterranean who lived in Europe. He was a hero of the antifascist resistance but also a pacifist. He will always be remembered as part of the existentialist circles of postwar Paris, which included Jean-Paul Sartre and Simone de Beauvoir, and yet he was an intensely private person. Camus was a celebrity with many lovers who liked to style himself after Humphrey Bogart. But he was also a serious intellectual and the second youngest recipient of the Nobel Prize for Literature. He was a problematical man. Yet there is something on which all agree: Camus was a writer of remarkable integrity, who lived an extraordinary life, and who offers a moral outlook that speaks to our time.[1]

Camus was born in 1913 in Algiers. His father had died during World War I and he grew up with his mother, who was deaf and suffered from a speech impediment, and his stern grandmother. His childhood was marked by silence and poverty. Luckily, he caught the attention of his public school teacher, Louis Germain, who became like a second father. Germain secured a set of scholarships for his precocious and poverty-stricken prodigy that, ultimately, led Camus to study at the university. Camus started out as a bohemian. His early essays dealt with everyday life: enjoying the sun and the beach, experiencing loneliness, and feelings of mortality. Soon enough, however, he became interested in the theater: he acted, directed, and began writing plays. In 1934, he married Simone Hie. She was a drug addict and, after numerous embarrassing episodes, they divorced. Camus then decided to marry Francine Faure—a mathematician with whom he later had twins. As the 1930s wore on, however, the bohemian became more explicitly political. Camus joined the Communist Party for a brief spell, and he wrote articles for *Alger Républicain* defending the Spanish Republic, the anti-fascist Popular Front, and the victims of colonial injustice and police torture in Algeria. His gripping editorials exposing incompetence and seeking European aid during the terrible Kabylian famine of 1939 created a sensation in Algiers and gave Camus his first taste of celebrity. But then, disgusted with its dogmatism, he quit the Communist Party.

Early in 1940, Camus found a job as a reporter with *Paris-Soir* and he decided to leave Algiers for Paris. He hated the gray gloom of the city, the cheap hotels, its grinding poverty, and the separation from his family. Concentration camps, mass murder, and war marked the age. Ethical limits were seemingly disintegrating. The world was becoming absurd, devoid of ultimate meaning, and thus plagued by moral relativism. Camus responded with three works that would endure. *The Stranger* (1942) celebrated the ability of an individual to remake his life in the shadow of death. *The Myth of Sisyphus* (1942) served as a philosophical meditation on suicide—an absurd response to an absurd world—and a rebellion against meaninglessness in the name of human dignity. These works inspired young people all over the world. Yet it is *Caligula*, written in 1938 but first performed only in 1945, that offers the deepest insight into Camus' future. Its main character is a half-crazed emperor obsessed with utopian ambitions and arbitrary power—and the absurdity of life. The play presents an ethic of political engagement as a response to this kind of unlivable world that anticipates Camus' fateful decision to join the French Resistance.

Camus went underground following the invasion of France by the Nazis. He edited *Combat,* and his articles made him famous throughout France. During this time, he became friends with Sartre and other legendary intellectuals who would dominate postwar intellectual life. Camus also fell in love with María Casares, the fine actress, now best remembered for her minor part in the classic film *Children of Paradise.* A daughter of the former Spanish prime minister Santiago Casares Quiroga who worked as a volunteer nurse during the Spanish Civil War while still hardly a teenager, she starred in a number of Camus' plays and often threatened to end their stormy affair over his stubborn refusal to leave his wife. But, whether as a lover or a friend, María Casares remained his constant companion. Intense friendships were forged in the cafés of Saint-Germain-des-Prés, the underground cultural events, the parties at people's homes, and the countless political meetings. Postwar Paris resonated with the themes that had occupied Camus: personal responsibility, political engagement, and the need to derive meaning from existence in the aftermath of Auschwitz. Reflection upon his experience in the French Resistance led Camus to write his wonderful novel *The Plague* (1947), which is an ode to solidarity, the courage of everyday people, and the need to rebel against an unjust world—and make it just a little less unjust.

Sartre and Camus worked together in an attempt to develop a political alternative to both capitalism and communism. But that failed. They fell out: Sartre looked East and Camus looked West. Amid the background of the Cold War, Camus published his meditation on murder as "the pathology of the age," *The Rebel* (1952), which was seen as an attack upon communist revolution and an endorsement of liberal social reform. A debate ensued and popular opinion believed that Camus got the worst of it. Sartre accused him of refusing to take sides in the anti-imperialist struggles underway in Algeria and Vietnam while skewering his insistence upon humanitarian ideals. Camus responded with a satirical novel, *The Fall* (1956), about the hypocrisy of self-styled bohemian revolutionaries. Neither really won the debate. Camus employed liberal ethics to mask the lack of an anti-imperialist political strategy, while Sartre trumpeted a self-proclaimed political realism that, while legitimately anti-imperialist, completely misconstrued the character of communist politics. That debate has passed us by. At the time, however, Sartre's charges seemed validated when Camus won the Nobel Prize for Literature in 1957 and, in his acceptance speech, condemned the terrorism of both imperialists and anti-imperialists in the ongoing conflict over Algerian independence.

Camus was believed to have cast a plague on all houses. He condemned torture, the death penalty, and other abuses of human rights. But many believed he was simply mouthing platitudes. His literary star dimmed with a few unremarkable collections of essays and short stories. Camus escaped into various love affairs—and he appeared to live off his fame. Yet, if Sartre won the battle, Camus won the war. No one realized that Camus was working on a new manuscript, *The First Man*, when he unexpectedly died in a car crash in 1960. That unfinished novel appeared in 1996, and it reinvigorated his literary reputation. Camus appeared on the verge of producing yet another masterpiece. In the aftermath of 9/11, new forms of the old mass pathology have been unleashed in many parts of the world. ISIS and Boko Haram employ the most hideous forms of terror in the name of a future caliphate, civil and proxy wars abound, millions of refugees are on the march, and states are collapsing with the help of external intervention. Camus' insistence upon linking means and ends, placing ethical limits on political action, is more than welcome today. No writer is as salient for a world seemingly bereft of cosmopolitanism and humanism than Albert Camus.

7

Immigrants and Refugees

Krisztian Simon Interviews Stephen Eric Bronner for the Hungarian and East European Blog Kettős Mérce

KRISZTIAN SIMON: In the United States more than half of the state governors say refugees are not welcome. And the anti-refugee and anti-Muslim sentiments also play a great role in the presidential campaign. How can we explain this attitude?

STEPHEN ERIC BRONNER: Anti-immigrant/anti-refugee attitudes in the United States have mostly been generated by the Republican Party and its far-right wing, crystallized around the Tea Party. This relatively small organization has had enormous electoral success at local and state levels, especially in the South and the Midwest. Whether significant elements of the Democratic Party, or the more than 46 percent of Americans who didn't vote in the national elections of 2012, identify with important aspects of the Tea Party's ideology is not as clear-cut as the media would have us believe. Anti-immigrant attitudes are interlaced with the more dogmatic elements of evangelicalism, xenophobia, provincialism, and traditional prejudices. A progressive policy on immigration is also only possible by expanding the welfare state. And this, of course, runs against Tea Party economic thinking. Little wonder that every leading candidate for the Republican presidential nomination in 2016 embraced anti-immigrant/anti-refugee sentiments to a greater or lesser degree—most notoriously, Donald Trump and Ted Cruz. It's important to note that Trump in particular received strong support from independent voters and that the Democratic Party is not immune from anti-immigrant prejudice. There is little political incentive for its more conservative members to act otherwise. Arabs don't vote, and they are poorly organized. Lack of knowledge about Islam and the Middle East, coupled with media obsessions over terror, only add to the problem. Worse: ethics (and especially cosmopolitan ethics) is always in short supply.

KS: When we spoke last year, you said that most bigots are hiding their bigotry, trying to legitimize their messages in one way or another, but when it comes to Muslims, I have the impression that they are not trying to make these messages more socially acceptable (or as the Germans would say, *salonfähig*). They just use the same old, very obvious tropes that the racists of the first half of the last century did (basically equating Islam with terrorism, or saying that the United States has to find a way to monitor all foreign people entering the country). Why is that?

SEB: Radical anti-Arab sentiment was triggered by 9/11, the American invasions of Afghanistan and Iraq, the lingering distrust and competition with Iran, and more recently—of course—Syria and ISIS. Actual conflict hardened previously embedded prejudices. Right-wing Americans believe that the United States is (literally!) at war with a single people ("Arabs") inspired by (a uniform) "Islam." It is a struggle between "us" and "them." Irish, Italians, and Jews were once seen as foreign intruders—but never as terrorist vanguards. They were not stereotyped in this way. Especially provincial bigots inspired by Islamophobia and anti-Arab prejudice are genuinely scared. They are horrified by the terrorism that occurred in Belgium, Paris, and elsewhere—and, perhaps just as important, the new cultural conflicts that have shaken Europe. Many believe that the United States already has its hands full with blacks and Latinos—allowing immigration would supposedly merely compound existing problems.

When considering Arabs: "they" have radically different customs, they worship differently, they speak a different language, and they are considered little more than barbarians sharpening their scimitars at the gates of civilization. In Europe and the United States, right-wing demagogues stoke the fear that their countries are being overrun and that traditional identities are being imperiled. Loose talk by conservative candidates and right-wing pundits about the impending introduction of Sharia law only adds fuel to the fire. This has led sixteen states in my country to ban it officially and Republican politicians in thirty-two states have proposed legislation condemning it. Most of those prejudiced against Muslims are quick to claim that they are not racists but that the United States is at "war" and that bans on Muslims entering the country are based on matters of security rather than racism. Most also (grudgingly) admit that not all Muslims are terrorists, or even that all Latino immigrants are "criminals" or "rapists." Yet, so far as they are concerned, most terrorists are Muslims and most immigrants are criminals. To keep out the deviants, these self-proclaimed "realists" insist, requires draconian measures that will (unfortunately) impact upon the majority of law-abiding Arabs and Latinos. Civil liberties have never been much of a concern for the far right and, today, anti-immigrant prejudice fits perfectly into an overall agenda intent upon weakening welfare programs and strengthening the national security state.

KS: Some U.S. newspapers and magazines draw parallels between the unwillingness to accept Jewish refugees from Germany and the rest of Europe in the 1930s (on the grounds that they might import communist ideologies to the United States) and the current situation. Do you think that these are well-founded parallels?

SEB: Some parallels are legitimate. Exaggeration, hysteria, and paranoia—anchored in projection—are apparent in both past and present attempts to exclude the foreigner. I suggested as much in my book *The Bigot* (Yale University Press 2015). Exaggeration concerning the threat to American identity is obvious insofar as seventy thousand is the cap per year, and President Obama is seeking asylum for ten thousand Syrian refugees—all told, a drop in the bucket. Similarly, for all its self-congratulation, the United States accepted only seventy-five thousand of the four hundred thousand Jews that sought to emigrate from Germany between 1933 and 1939. Immigration again became a major theme in the Republican primaries of 2016 and, in fact, Donald Trump first became a political force with his sensational calls to ban all Muslim immigrants and build a "thousand-mile" wall along the Mexican border. It is not all that dissimilar from "America Firsters'" feelings about the Jews. Hysteria was evident in both cases—and the real situation was ignored.

Admittedly, the ideologies justifying exclusion were a bit different. But paranoia was evident in both cases. There were rumors about a Jewish world conspiracy, and Henry Ford had the notorious *Protocols of Zion* translated into English. Jews were also seen as communists, and the idea of "Jewish Bolshevism" was not confined to Germany. Today, bigots claim that Muslims are taking over the United States and threatening its freedoms. Yet ironically, it was not domestic communists who actually threatened America's freedoms but the House Un-American Activities Committee and McCarthyism. And, of course, whereas Muslims are accused of "invading" the United States, it was the United States that actually bombed and invaded Afghanistan and Iraq, thereby virtually destroying those nations and creating cultural havoc, while leaving millions dead, wounded, and exiled. That is the projection I was speaking about. In any event, whether in Europe or the United States, the implications of anti-Jewish prejudices then and anti-Arab prejudices now basically amount to the same thing: condemning the majority of refugees to lives of misery—or worse.

KS: When we look at the percentage of foreign-born people as part of their populations, we can see that many countries in the EU (e.g., Germany, Austria, Belgium) have a greater percentage of the foreign-born in their population than the United States. Still, the United States sees itself as a nation of immigrants, while most European countries refuse to define themselves as countries of immigration. So what can we infer from this? Has the United States ceased to be an open and welcoming place to immigrants, or are European countries more open to newcomers than it would seem just based on the rhetoric of their politicians?

SEB: The Statue of Liberty has inscribed on it the words "Give me your tired and your poor, your huddled masses yearning to be free." Immigrants from all over the world have come to the United States, settled, and made a life. To be sure: each wave of immigration was greeted with prejudices and stereotypes that were often interchangeable while "the American creed" is clearly associated with Anglo-Protestant values. Racism has indeed proven the "cancer" of American life (as W. E. B. Du Bois noted) and the easiest road to assimilation has always been reserved for white European peoples. African Americans obviously did not come of their own volition, while both Hispanics and even Asians had to endure virtual slave-like conditions working the fields or on railroads in the West during the nineteenth century and then, later, internment during World War II.

Old-fashioned racism targeting African Americans today bleeds over into the prejudices directed against Hispanics and Arabs seeking refuge in the United States. Interestingly, Samuel Huntington targeted the Arab world in *The Clash of Civilizations* and Hispanics in the sequel, *Who Are We?* Few thinkers are taken as seriously by the mainstream political establishment. But still there is no reason for Europeans to feel smug: America has no Arab ghettos (*banlieus*) as in Paris, and it is not as if Europe has exactly welcomed either Arabs or Jews or any number of other groups in their times of need.

KS: Do you think Europe and the United States expect too much from immigrants?

SEB: I'm not quite sure what that means. Most immigrant groups have produced solid hard-working citizens who live in ethnic neighborhoods, as in the case of Arabs living in Jersey City and Paterson, New Jersey, or Dearborn, Michigan. They are patriotic, law-abiding, and mostly grateful for the opportunities provided them in their new homeland. They have assimilated—and that is to be expected. But it is also true that old habits die hard, and it would be foolish to expect that immigrants simply discard their heritage. There is also no reason why they should. Whether ethnic or religious or national loyalty gains the upper hand, however, is not always a foregone conclusion. The existential importance of identity, and the feeling of belonging to a particular group, are strengthened or weakened depending on the degree to which immigrants feel accepted by the broader culture. It is common knowledge, for example, that American counter-terrorist agencies rely a great deal on information from the Muslim community when it comes to the activities of Muslim terrorists. Intolerant rhetoric directed against immigrants, in this regard, can only prove counter-productive. Growing Islamophobia and outrageous expressions of anti-Arab sentiments give immigrants incentives to circle the wagons around their communities, and it helps turn the bigot's prejudices into self-fulfilling prophecies. Tolerance and generosity are not identical with the formalities associated with the liberal rule of law. It is worth remembering that loyalty, acceptance, and tolerance are all two-way streets.

KS: What kind of integration should we expect from people who want to come to our countries and settle down? How much of their heritage should they leave behind? As an American born to refugees from Germany, you speak perfect German, and when you're in Germany there are probably lots of people who believe you are local or from some other part of Germany. We see this as normal (at least now, in 2015, we do—hopefully). In the case of a U.S. or European Muslim, however, lots of people would find this suspicious. Is this a double standard? Or does it only indicate that people are always suspicious, and they need time, lots of time, to get used to people who have different habits from theirs?

SEB: America was not so much a melting pot as a salad with different ingredients, although as I just said, that too is changing. Neighborhoods were distinct and separate from one another and, whatever the misplaced nostalgia, they were quite provincial. Yes, it is true what you say about my background: I was born in a neighborhood composed almost exclusively of German Jewish exiles and I learned German as a child. Unlike children of other immigrant groups, however, I am white, my parents were working-class people, and of course my primary language was English—and that made things much easier. The real issue you raise is, I think, more difficult for other kinds of immigrants, namely, what can they do to erase the prejudices of bigots who consider themselves "real" Americans or Europeans?

Immigrants can organize themselves into voting blocs and create lobbies or interest groups to strengthen their political influence. In this way they can change the perception of the mainstream, improve their economic prospects, and enter the public sphere. When it comes to changing the bigot's views, however, it is another matter entirely. That is because his stereotypes have nothing to do with the lives of real Jews, African Americans, Latinos, or Arabs. The bigot mentally constructs the "other" to justify his preconceived opinions, and usually his stereotypes are easily transferable from one group to another. The bigot also usually hates in clusters. Though bigotry can intensify or diminish in different circumstances, one thing is constant: prejudice is about the opinions of the bigot, not the lived life of his target.

Part II

Murderous Impulses

Mass oppression is so much a part of human history that it is often greeted with indifference. Not every such event constitutes "genocide," a word coined amid the shock of Auschwitz and the Gulag—nor should that be necessary to inspire outrage. Mass oppression militates against the "compare and contrast" question on an exam. Ideology and interest underpin every case, however, as should become evident from "Learning the Ropes." But nowhere are ideological and material interests more in play than the Israeli-Palestinian conflict and, in particular, how to understand the plight of Gaza. This section treats mass oppression from a number of different angles but, in most of the instances under consideration, there is an almost studied ignorance—other than by groups that experienced its impact. Few in the West know anything about the "garbage people" of Cairo or the national memories associated with the mass murders of Circassians at Sochi in the nineteenth century. Of course, mass oppression can also (even indirectly) hit closer to home as in Iraq, Syria, or even in the violence suffered mostly by subaltern groups in the United States. Either way, however, I hope this section will foster a more general sensitivity to the phenomenon of mass oppression not only when it occurs but whenever it first becomes a possibility.

8

Learning the Ropes

Remarks on the Ideological Preconditions for Genocide

Genocide does not simply "happen." Opportunism, indifference, political ambitions, conformism, and fear all play a role. But more important perhaps is the learned prejudice of the masses that ultimately legitimate the perverse and horrific demands of mass murder. Genocide does not require a modern state, an advanced economy, or gas chambers. It can occur under free-market capitalism as in the case of slavery and the extermination of Native Americans in the United States, state planning as in the case of communism, or economic underdevelopment as in the case of Cambodia or Rwanda. Fixating on the cog in the machine, the small-minded bureaucrat, the Neanderthal, or the "little man" unconcerned with ethical reflection, is also misleading. The "go along to get along" attitude is insufficient for mass murder. Fanatical prejudices that demonize a victim need strengthening and pre-reflective judgments call for justification. For that very reason, it is always best to choose a victim lacking or with limited organized political representation. Reactionary traditions, habits, and institutional forms of education thus become crucial for the genocidal enterprise. Peppered with emotional extremism, they congeal into a dynamic of hate that once triggered is difficult to temper or restrain.

Of course, prejudice does not inevitably lead to the gas chambers—even if creating the gas chambers requires the existence of fanatical prejudice. Decisive for understanding genocide is the mind of the perpetrator rather than the lived life of the intended victim, whether the Jew, the Trotskyite, the immigrant, or (like the Aborigine or the Native American) the original inhabitant of a given territory. Or, put in more academic terms, the key to unlocking any given genocide is the specific constellation of hatred internalized by the genocidal agent. What turns a simple authoritarian or bigot into the fanatical perpetrator of prejudice is the justifications by which all empathy or compassion for the intended victims is denied. This explains the insistent use of vilifying metaphors depicting them as inhuman or, quite often, as vermin. The learned reduction of the human to the inhuman brings with it a learned indifference to suffering. Himmler could note in an address to his concentration camp officials in Poznań on October 4, 1943, that they actually were the victims (rather than those sent to the ovens) since no pity would be given to them but rather the Jews whose innate evil demanded their annihilation. Thus, the importance of projection that enables the perpetrator to feel justified in *actually* performing the dreadful acts in the present that his victims will supposedly perform in the future.

Nazis during the 1920s and 1930s insisted that Jews were enmeshed in a conspiracy bent on fostering chaos through assassinations, poisoning the public sphere, instituting terror, turning education into self-serving propaganda, and leading the world into yet another war. Of course, it was actually Nazis and groups like the Thule Society that were engaged in a conspiracy, celebrated violence, assassinated progressive politicians like Walther Rathenau, propagated the fabricated *Protocols of Zion*, and demanded a new war of revenge to exculpate the German defeat in 1918. Psychological projection was similarly manifest among Stalinists. Not their mostly fictitious and powerless internal enemies but they themselves engaged in conspiracies, plotted assassinations, subverted the military, sabotaged industrial production, unleashed purges, perverted justice, rewrote history, and helped the Nazis begin World War II.

The more unchecked the psychological projection, the more intense the hate and the less necessary the need for rationally justifying actions. Only the genocidal agent is fully aware of the evil being planned since, after all, the demonized image of his enemy only exists in his imagination. The tautology is obvious. But this experiential "knowledge" turns him into a member of the elite. Only he and his comrades recognize the enemies to their community. He and his friends can even view themselves as heroes insofar as they alone are fighting against so vast a conspiracy. Everything is now permitted the fanatic. Unfettered action becomes tied to absolute acceptance of the imperatives dictated by fate and the religious/political institution incarnating it. As Hegel knew, license and domination are actually flip sides of the same coin. Thus, the Nazis could quite legitimately interpret the "night of the pogroms" (*Kristallnacht*) as a form of "organized spontaneity."

Hitler, Stalin, and Mao all understood that genocidal hatred could be taught. An appropriate narrative is thus required that identifies the enemy with absolute evil, that gives no credence to the critical faculty, and that rests on the "coordination" (*Gleichschaltung*) of all media and institutions in targeting the "Other." The ideological aim of such propaganda is not simply to develop sentiments of hatred or even turn some inchoate mass into a genocidal agent. It is also not merely a matter of heaping invective on the intended victim. The real aim is to highlight his resilience, the ongoing character of the threat that he poses, and the need for constant vigilance. The Jew or the Trotskyist may appear powerless and defeated, but the Nazi or the Stalinist understands that this is only a disguise.

The genocidal agent is always preparing for a preemptive strike. Recognizing the limitless power of the enemy, he becomes the enforcer of "destiny," "fate," or "inevitability." Guilt is eliminated, or at least lessened, as the need to follow orders without question turns into an ethical imperative. The future mass murderer believes himself the hero of his own drama. Little wonder, then, that the intended victim is depicted as a demiurge or as a natural force, whose evil emanates from the stereotypical traits embedded within him. Fixed stereotypical traits, myths emanating from the mist of history, and unshakeable intuitive judgments justify the fanatic's arbitrary exercise of power. The intended victim can become anything that his future murderer wants him to be. Nazis identified the Jew with the capitalist, the communist, the socialist, the bohemian, the cultural degenerate, and a host of other social images. Conflicts of interests and beliefs between these groups are irrelevant: the Jew is pulling the strings everywhere. Nor was it any different with respect to the endless array of ideologically diverse saboteurs and plotters united only by their hatred of the world that Stalin was building. In both cases, an evil "essence" was holding together the diverse disguises in which the enemy appeared. It is necessary to rip away the masks. Then it will become evident that the enemy is what he is. Dialogue is useless. That essence can never be eradicated—unless it is physically eradicated.

The end justifies the means given the psychological projection, the hysteria, fears, and the exaggerated ambitions inspired by the enemy. That nothing justifies the end other than the means used to achieve it is irrelevant. Embracing the genocidal cause is possible only by ignoring the need for exercising the critical faculty and insisting upon some plausible connection between ends and means. The religious or teleological end requires no empirical evidence that it is actually being reached through the means employed. Against the elder Marx and his orthodox followers, for example, Stalin insisted that terror must drastically increase and the "contradictions" become more "acute" as the achievement of socialism grows nearer. Those who disagreed—or, better, who lacked the same degree of fanaticism—were traitors to the faith, by definition, and thus could be dealt with summarily as circumstances dictated. In this way, the oxymoronic character of genocidal thinking is striking: it always privileges a self-serving yet perversely principled abdication of personal responsibility.

Ideological motivations for genocide are ultimately based on ignited passions. Insofar as perpetrators rely on intuition, experience, faith, and tradition to justify their motivational passions—their beliefs, myths, and stereotypes—they become difficult to engage in rational discourse. The passions define their identity. Ernst Bloch liked to quote the words of an intelligent acquaintance who became a Nazi and, when confronted with counter-arguments, replied: "One does not die for a program that one understands but for a program that one loves." For the impassioned adherent to a dogma, there is nothing provisional about truth, and bothering to logically justify claims threatens the certainty required to carry out the genocidal act. Opportunism and ambition, of course, infect the majority of those engaged in perpetrating mass murder. But the ideologically committed genocidal agent is marked by an instilled toughness, a cynical anti-intellectual attitude, and a simple laziness of mind. He is always right and always superior to his intended victim if only because he feels that he is.

The fanatic knows what he knows and that knowledge is unassailable almost by definition. There is nothing to learn. Criticisms targeting the murky assumptions of potentially genocidal ideologies or the value of civil liberties and tolerance will probably have little impact. But there are also those who, so to speak, hate in good faith. Their prejudices stem from genuine ignorance or ideological manipulation rather than malevolence or fear of losing their material and existential privileges. They are not quite fanatics or ready for violence. Enlightenment thinking with its emphasis upon critical reflection, reciprocity, social justice, tolerance, and the liberal rule of law might just put them on the defensive. There are enough of those people around. Reaching even a minority of them would help marginalize the motivating passions and psychological inclinations of the genocidal actor. And, after all, isn't that the primary purpose of any liberal education with a cosmopolitan intent?

9

Gaza on My Mind

Old Hopes, Mistaken Assumptions, and New Ideas on the Israeli-Palestinian Conflict

> At the moment of their departure they left me with thorns of remembrance and never returned.
>
> —Mahmoud Darwish

Terms like "liberal education" or "cosmopolitan intent" don't exactly leap to mind when thinking about Gaza. Yet hopes for peace were soaring in 2004 when Prime Minister Ariel Sharon of Israel began evacuating eight thousand Israeli settlers. As Western newspapers depicted wailing Israeli settlers, bemoaning their betrayal while waiting for government checks to soften their move from Gaza, the evacuation was accompanied by nearly universal acclamation. It seemed like the first step in the creation of a Palestinian State. Only a year later, however, those hopes vanished. Control was kept by Israel over the roads, airspace, electricity, and borders of Gaza. With the approval of the United States, fourteen thousand more Israeli settlements are on the ground, thus effectively freezing the prospect of an independent Palestine. The Palestinians were not fooled—Israeli withdrawal from Gaza was not the prelude to a peace deal but to further Zionist expansion and redrawing the borders of a "Greater Israel."

In 2016, peace now looks further away than ever. Western media embraced the Israeli version of events: that it had no choice but to invade Gaza in response to consistent violations of a cease-fire by Hamas, a cease-fire that this "terrorist" organization refused to extend, and the importance of standing up to terrorism. But the deal was that, if Hamas ceased its rocket fire, Israel would ease its embargo: Hamas did radically reduce its attacks and Israel only strengthened its blockage; Hamas declared itself willing to rekindle negotiations; Israel closed the door. Hamas may have acted less out of calculation than bravado, and crude organizational self-interest, but Israeli leaders were motivated far less by international concerns with opposing terror in order to further the pursuit of peace than gaining ground against their rivals in the February elections.[1]

With the Israeli aerial assault on Gaza in December of 2008, following the closing of its borders, a humanitarian crisis arose that many feel put another nail in the coffin of a "two-state solution" to the Israeli-Palestinian conflict. Thirteen hundred Gazans were killed including well over two hundred children as against thirteen Israelis and three civilians. One and a half million Gazans remain cramped into a coastal strip of 140 square miles of land that is bereft of resources and infrastructure. Forty-nine percent of Gazan citizens are unemployed, the World Food Program estimates that 35 to 60 percent of Gazan agriculture has been ruined, 80 percent earn less than $2 per day, one hundred thousand have abandoned their homes, twenty-two thousand buildings have been destroyed, and the damages according to UNICEF now amount to roughly $2 billion. Electricity food, fuel, water, medical supplies, and sanitation services have been dramatically reduced. In short, Gaza is in ruins.[2]

There is no need to stoke the flames with misplaced historical analogies that compare what is happening in Gaza with the "holocaust." Things are bad enough and Gazans are undoubtedly feeling a sense of déjà vu. Many are descended from the six thousand expelled from Israel in what is called the "catastrophe" (*Nakba*) of 1947–1948. That was the first time Israel invaded Gaza; it happened again in 1956 and 1967 and, most recently, in 2006. But today is not yesterday. Palestine is now both geographically and ideologically divided. Elections that had been demanded by then–U.S. secretary of state Condoleezza Rice and Mahmoud Abbas, whose Fatah party controlled the West Bank, proved a disaster. With its base of support in Gaza, Hamas won 43 percent of the vote and new influence over the Palestinian National Authority Legislature. In March 2007, Hamas and Fatah formed a national unity government that was ready to negotiate a long-term ceasefire with Israel. But the Gazans had apparently voted the wrong way. Israel and the "quartet" of allegedly concerned peacemakers—the European Union, the United Nations, Russia, and the United States—refused to recognize or engage in negotiations with a government that included a "terrorist" organization.

Attempts to form a unity government between these two branches of the Palestinian Authority collapsed amid fighting in the streets between Hamas and Fatah in Gaza that King Abdullah of Saudi Arabia termed "more dangerous than Israeli aggression" (*The Economist*, 24 January 2009, 51). Fatah remains notorious for its corruption and Hamas has taken to assassinating supposed collaborators in Gaza. Conflict between the two organizations has raged over the interminable character and negligible results of negotiations with Israel, and—perhaps most importantly—a profound division concerning the future of Palestine. Hamas was not invited to the Annapolis Conference that President George W. Bush put together in 2008 to address the Israeli-Palestinian conflict.[3] Suspicion concerning the quartet's commitment to peace was only compounded by its tacit endorsement of Israel's blockade that gradually tightened after a truce was established in June of 2008 and that was accompanied by a suspension of suicide bombings, and even rocket fire into Israel. The cease-fire failed. Desperate to assert its organizational interests as the representative of the Palestinians, provoked by the killing of its partisans and the mass arrests of its supporters in the West Bank, Hamas once again began its rocket fire on Ashkelon, Beersheba, and Sderot. This problematic decision on the part of Hamas and its allies like Islamic Jihad demonstrates how the current *Palestinian state in waiting* lacks a single sovereign institution with what Max Weber termed a "legitimate monopoly over the means of coercion." Three states—not two—still define the current crisis in Israeli-Palestinian relations—thereby dramatically complicating the pursuit of a just peace and a "two-state solution." Israel could have renegotiated the truce by opening the borders of Gaza to humanitarian aid and the basic necessities of life. Nevertheless, its decision on Gaza was shaped by its broader tactic of stalling and delaying negotiations with Fatah on the fate of the West Bank and a Palestinian state.

The seemingly endless and mind-numbing negotiations with Fatah enervated the peace movement. In the election of 2009, the coalition of Ehud Barak's Labor Party and the centrist Kadima Party run by Tzipi Livni and Ehud Olmert understood that the primary threat they faced came from Benjamin Netanyahu of the staunchly anti-concession and militarist Likud Party. They saw an opportunity and took it. Responding to the rocket fire of Hamas seemed a way for Labor and Kadima to steal the thunder from their right-wing rival. They had little to lose in mounting an attack. To be sure: the United States and the rest of the quartet publicly chastised Israel for expanding its settlements and publicly praised Fatah for its "moderation."

But the Israeli government knew that it would suffer no curtailment of economic or military aid. Its leaders also knew that an invasion would secure the division of Gaza from the West Bank, compromise the character of the existing Palestinian state in waiting, and shatter the (always fragile) unity of the Palestinian enterprise for national self-determination. Perhaps they even anticipated an added benefit: the savagery of its assault and the magnitude of the humanitarian crisis in Gaza unleashed by Israel might actually deflect concern away from expanding Israeli settlement elsewhere and the creation of an independent Palestine.[4]

Israeli losses were insignificant both in terms of casualties and infrastructure. Some suggested that Israeli actions imperiled its most basic strategic needs: the protection of its citizens, its deterrent power, its international support, and the prospect of peace. But this is rather naïve. Israeli citizens were well protected and they remain so—at least relative to the Palestinians. And, even should Hamas rockets strike deeper into Israel, this would only build national resolve and unity. The real implications were somewhat different. Ironically, the "realists" and "pragmatists" like Livni and Olmert created the ideological and practical preconditions for the success of Benjamin Netanyahu as surely as mainstream Republicans under George W. Bush set the stage for the Tea Party and, ultimately, Donald Trump as the standard bearer of the GOP in 2016.

Israel has always relied on its ability to launch preemptive strikes and military interventions—and, concerns over international support notwithstanding, there is no reason to assume that its behavior will change. Saudi Arabia has refused to place an embargo on Israel and relations with Egypt, Jordan, and Turkey remain firm. That Qatar and Mauritania have suspended relations will surely not produce sleepless nights in Israel. If it were the United States, of course, that would be another matter. But, while there has been a shift in sentiment regarding the Israeli-Palestinian conflict, this should not be overestimated. The Obama administration criticized Israeli settlement policy and dawdling over peace negotiations. In 2016, however, it gave Israel a ten-year $38 billion military trade package. Existing boycotts and divestment strategies are more symbolic than real, and that is also the case with the countless resolutions by the United Nations. Right-wing Zionists have also always assumed that the *goyim* are untrustworthy (if not latent anti-Semites) and that the creation of an independent Palestine will burden Israel with an enduring security problem. They take the Israeli establishment at its word—and ignore the obvious reality: today, even less than yesterday, the Israeli political elite (beyond party affiliation) has no real interest in an equitable peace with the Palestinians.

Everything becomes clear once the image of Israel as the nation intent upon securing peace is called into question—and Hamas is seen as (for its own purposes) playing into the hands of the imperialist enemy. Saudi Arabia put forward a plan that would have given formal recognition from all members of the Arab League in exchange for withdrawal to pre-1967 borders, a partition of Jerusalem, a halt in settlement construction, and some recognition of the "right of return" or compensation for Palestinians living in exile.[5] Virtually every activist and scholar concerned with establishing a two-state solution knows that these are the parameters in which it must take place. The basis for any future "security" of Israel lies in formal recognition of its sovereignty; Jerusalem is already partitioned de facto and its religious diversity requires formal expression and guarantees;[6] land swaps with relatively tiny amounts of territory involved can deal with current settlements but, obviously, the possibility of bringing about a sovereign Palestine must preclude further settlements; and, as for the contentious "right of return," plans could be developed that would provide monetary compensation for those choosing not to return. The point is that the basic issues underpinning a settlement have already been articulated both specifically and in an integrated fashion. Whatever its public pronouncements, however, the Israeli right simply has no wish to see a Palestinian state. It views Zionist settlements as steps toward building a "greater Israel," threatens armed violence should the state attempt to remove them or transfer their territory to the Arabs, and insists that Jewish control over Jerusalem is nonnegotiable. Thus, what appears as a tactic in stalling negotiations is actually a strategy: delay negotiations on any pretext, preserve the status quo, and claim ever more land in order to change the facts on the ground and develop a greater Israel.

Blocking any prospects for peace was the real motive behind the invasion of Gaza—and Israel is the primary culprit for the misery that transpired. Its callous disregard of international law, its imperialist arrogance, and its disproportionate use of violence in seeking "security" are undeniable. It is Israel that began the attack, it is Israel that engaged in what the late Baruch Kimmerling has termed "sociocide," and it is Israel that must bear responsibility for its actions. There is a legitimate case to be made that those who authorized the outrages in Gaza should be forced to stand trial for crimes against humanity. All of this together produced a swing in world opinion favorable to Hamas if not necessarily a bandwagon effect. But still, too many well-meaning people have been wildly naive in estimating Hamas, condemning moderation as "treason," and treating the two-state solution as an anachronism. They insist, whatever the problems, Hamas is at least "doing something"!

But what is Hamas actually doing? It has provided social services for the residents of Gaza while under occupation and constantly imperiled by military attack. It has represented the spirit of militancy while carrying on an internecine and subterranean war with Fatah. It appears as the principled opponent of Israeli imperialism—but its vacillation on recognizing Israel and its ambivalence on the two-state solution, coupled with its moral justification of violence and anti-Semitic rhetoric, has an institutionally self-serving quality and further legitimates the Israeli right. The two fit hand in glove. Hamas has strengthened its role in the Palestinian Authority as surely as the Israeli right has secured control over its country's political landscape. Both dance around the need to recognize the other and the "two-state solution" by essentially claiming that they will come on board if the majority of the citizenry endorses it—even as each does everything possible to undermine the possibility of achieving that consensus.

With Israel justifying an imperialist policy as part of the war on terror, and the suffering of Gaza, Hamas is acting like a shyster lawyer grabbing the limelight while an impoverished client bears the costs of a seemingly endless trial. Its endorsement of launching rockets into Israel as a form of retribution for Israeli aggression not only undermines Fatah and Palestinian solidarity, and provides its enemy with yet another excuse for breaking off dialogue, but also sabotages the prospects of a Palestinian state in waiting and any possible improvement in the lives of Gazan citizens. Since it was formed in 1987, the identity of Hamas has rested on its Islamic convictions and its opposition to a two-state solution to the Israeli-Palestinian conflict. Compromising these pillars of its institutional identity would leave Hamas as merely a slightly more radical version of Fatah. The situation is no different with regard to its insistence on the illegitimacy of precedents for settling the Israeli-Palestinian conflict (including United Nations Security Council Resolution 242).

Neither Israel nor the United States should be giving lectures on the dangers of missionary zeal, violence, or the sanctity of UN resolutions. Hamas is not monolithic and there are clear openings for negotiations. Hamas has never tried to impose Sharia law, it has (in fact) often negotiated with Israel in the past, it is willing to consider a cease-fire of up to fifty years with Israel, and its leadership has openly stated that a two-state solution is acceptable should the majority of Palestinians agree in a free vote. Hints that project a new and more pragmatic attitude, however, are always balanced by outbursts of the more old-fashioned rhetoric and violence. Should Hamas supplant Fatah (which is entirely possible), the more pragmatic perspective will probably grow stronger. Until then, however, Hamas has its identity to protect, its fight with Fatah to win, and its own interest in delaying any resolution to the conflict. What Hamas now seeks could have been gained without a rocket being launched against Israel or a bomb being dropped on Gaza. Were there something more to the policy of Hamas than organizational self-interest, indeed, it would not now be willing to reengage Fatah and cease its rocket fire in exchange for a partial opening of the Gazan borders and a withdrawal of Israeli troops—or, to put it more simply, reestablish the status quo ante (*New York Times*, 14 February 2009).

Many analysts have noted that there is no military solution to the Israeli-Palestinian conflict. But what if delaying any solution is itself seen as the solution? That is the strategy of both the Israeli right and Hamas—and Gaza has made abundantly clear how they reinforce and legitimate one another. Each is defined by what it opposes. Each also pursues its organizational interest with self-righteous zealotry and without the slightest regard either for its own base or the broader Palestinian constituency. Each has contributed to creating the roadblock that undermines the possibility of peace beyond the stated desires of majorities in both Israel and Palestine that seek an end to the conflict and the creation of two sovereign states. It is as if extremists on both sides, unwilling or unable to articulate a strategy linking means and ends, had a veto over the will of the majority and a meaningful policy.

Neither the Israeli right nor Hamas is going away. The roadblock that they created calls not merely for a new intervention by the United States, but a reevaluation of mistaken assumptions and failed policies by their own supporters. Kant once wrote that "who wills the end necessarily wills the means thereto." If the creation of a Palestinian state is truly the strategic goal of the United States, then it must employ tactics that will further its creation—or, at least, buttress the Palestinian state in waiting. Two implications derive from this: 1) American foreign policy must foster cooperation between Hamas and Fatah, and 2) American foreign policy must insist not merely upon the security of Israel, but of Palestine as well. Acting on these two ideas would mark a dramatic shift in outlook: Hamas has traditionally been branded as a terrorist organization, and excluded from all negotiations sponsored by the quartet, while preserving the security of Israel has been used to justify its military control over Palestine and its interventions that take place with regularity and impunity.

Commitment to these two aforementioned goals rests on the willingness by the United States to articulate economic incentives for Hamas and sanctions on Israel. Only in this way is it possible to think about altering political behavior that has become entrenched and that undermines the prospect of peace. So far, however, American policy in the Middle East has rested on the opposite set of assumptions: placing economic sanctions on Hamas and giving economic incentives to Israel for extending the conflict. Such an approach only fortifies the existing imbalance of power between Israel and Palestine—and, just as important, the most reactionary tendencies within the two camps.

Economic and military aid is a specific tool for exerting influence and, to that extent, rethinking the conditions for its employment becomes important for establishing new connections between American strategy and tactics in the region. According to the Congressional Research Service's 2007 report "U.S. Foreign Aid to Israel," $6.8 million per day is being spent on military aid to Israel—not to mention another $1.4 billion yearly in guaranteed loans. In 2008, the Bush administration demanded a 12 percent increase in aid to Israel. As for Palestine (or, better, Fatah), by contrast, it received $3 million. Worth considering is that Israel essentially was given this aid without any preconditions, whereas adherence to nonviolence, the recognition of Israel, and the "two-state solution" was demanded of Fatah. It is also worth considering that Egypt received roughly $2 billion in military-economic aid, while Jordan was given about $500,000,000. Both Egypt and Jordan have negotiated separate peace treaties with Israel, refused to support an oil embargo on Israel, and have been complicit in isolating Gaza.

Would Israeli behavior change if American aid were tied to achieving certain benchmarks? The same question can be asked with respect to Hamas. Would its behavior change if it were offered economic aid and integrated into the peace process undertaken by the Palestinian state in waiting? Perhaps, or perhaps not, but the likelihood is far better than if Hamas is treated as it has been by the United States. Some believe that the United States should simply cut aid to Israel or—without simply referencing Israel—refuse to provide aid for any nation or movement whose actions contradict international law. There is a certain moral power to these last two arguments. That is also the case with the decision by the Obama administration to provide $300 million in humanitarian aid for nongovernmental organizations working in Gaza—should Israel choose to open the border—and another $600 million to the Palestinian Authority (*New York Times*, 24 February 2009).

All these proposals, however, leave Hamas and Gaza out of the mix. The United States and the quartet need to recognize this reality. They will have to shape their policies with an eye not merely on the "security" of Israel but that of Gaza and the West Bank. Perhaps negotiations in the future will involve three "states" rather than two. Rethinking the use of foreign aid in the region by making it available to all the major regional actors, and linking aid to specific and achievable benchmarks in pursuit of peace, is one way of addressing this issue. It bridges the chasm separating strategy from tactics and ends from means in American foreign policy.

How realistic is any of this? Determining the benchmarks is nothing more than a technical matter if the Saudi plan is used as an objective point of reference. Also, there has already been a marked change in the relatively unqualified support that Israel has received from the United States since 1967. Criticism of Israel by the Obama administration has increased not only due to the plight of the Palestinians, especially in Gaza, but the expansion of settlements and unwillingness to negotiate in good faith. In spite of powerful lobbying organizations like AIPAC, and the uncritical support offered Israel by politicians in both parties, Democratic voters overwhelmingly opposed the Israeli invasion of Gaza (31–55%), though Republican voters supported it (62–27%).[7] This shows a shift in public opinion on the Middle East. Yet political discussion in the United States still seems focused more on Israeli than on a robust debate concerning American regional interests. Articulating those interests offers an opportunity for progressives in the political establishment. Sending a congressional delegation to Gaza would prove a step in the right direction—but only a step. But the new ten-year $38 billion aid package for Israel is clearly a step backward. Old ways of thinking become stronger in periods of political stalemate. There is a need for new ideas—even though for now they can only take speculative form.

10

Netanyahu's Rhetoric

It has often been said that truth is the first victim of politics. Looking backward, politicians have mostly tried to hide or veil or qualify their fabrications. Lying as an end unto itself was generally left to totalitarians and other ideological fanatics: Hitler, Stalin, or Mao. They used propaganda as forms of political education, information, and—above all—as mobilizing strategies for realizing various strategic purposes. But the totalitarian monopoly on employing this kind of rhetorical consolidation seems to have reached its end. The strategy has now spread to Western democracies where truth is not so much irrelevant as impotent. Lying has become an acceptable form of political provocation that builds upon itself. Unreasonable fear can easily be provoked, hatred and ignorance, too, by demagogues intent upon "us" circling the wagons against either an internal or external enemy.

America has Trump (and his rivals) in the Republican Party. France has Marine Le Pen, Germany has Lutz Bachmann, Greece is stuck with the fascist Golden Dawn, Jobbik's partisans are busy in Hungary, Italy had Berlusconi, and it would be impolite to exclude Israeli prime minister Benjamin Netanyahu from the club. Each forges a particular combination of his myths, stereotypes, and prejudices. They are unconcerned about empirical evidence, whether it pertains to their particular enemy, whether Arabs, Jews, or Roma. The left often laughs over the demagoguery. But it isn't funny. Outlandish xenophobic and racist claims are not simply products of ignorance or misspeaking. Intelligence is less the issue than the cynical attitude of a con man that every demagogue possesses.

Truth has been turning into simply one "opinion" among others. There are just too many spin doctors, too much infotainment, and too many sensationalist websites to inhibit a politician on the make from saying whatever serves his purpose. Netanyahu is nothing special in that regard. Sometimes explicitly, and other times implicitly, he identifies Palestinians with Nazis and, as a logical consequence, Israelis with Jews murdered in the

Holocaust. In late October 2015, for example, Netanyahu claimed that Nazis were ready to allow Jewish emigration to Palestine, or someplace else like Madagascar, had not the Grand Mufti al-Husseini of Jerusalem intervened. He apparently convinced Hitler in a meeting with him on November 28, 1941, that such a plan was impractical. It would be far better to "burn" the Jews and thereby "eliminate" the problem entirely.

Of course, this is not a matter of bringing up a new understanding of Nazis politics for academic discussion. Aside from the fact that there is nothing new here,[1] Netanyahu meant to suggest that Arabs in general and Palestinians in particular were complicit in the Holocaust—on the basis of a conversation. European anti-Semitism in the first decades of the twentieth century had its political parties, philosophers, artists, magazines, and academic curricula. It was one (albeit not particularly respectable) worldview among others. Anti-Semitism could be found almost anywhere but especially in Vienna where Hitler spent so much time prior to World War I. He knew the racist arguments generated by Houston Stewart Chamberlain's popular *Foundations of the Nineteenth Century* and Richard Wagner's "The Jews and Modern Music," and he listened to the anti-Semitic theories of his "court philosopher," Alfred Rosenberg. In short, Hitler already considered the Jew a form of "racial tuberculosis" as early as 1919. He was also enthusiastic about the *Protocols of Zion* with its fabricated vision of a world Jewish conspiracy, and his Nazi Party endorsed the psychotic Julius Streicher, editor of the anti-Semitic rag-sheet *Der Stürmer*, who missed no opportunity to portray Jews as vermin, sexually depraved, and the incarnation of evil. Indeed, *Mein Kampf* explicitly made the case for the genocidal elimination of Jews.

All these works and theories basically treated Jews as an alien and inherently evil presence at worst—or, at best, as what Heinrich von Treitschke, the famous historian, called "our misfortune." Hitler had no need of the undoubtedly anti-Semitic Grand Mufti, whom he barely knew, to develop either his views or his policies on anti-Semitism or Zionism. And Hitler certainly did not look to Islam for meaningful practical assistance: it was obviously not the Palestinians who ran the trains, organized the delivery of inmates, constructed the ovens, or supervised the camps. Netanyahu knew that his statement about the Grand Mufti was nothing more than a symbolic provocation and, quickly enough in the face of public outcry (but with a knowing wink), he retracted what he said and admitted that the Nazis themselves were responsible for Auschwitz.

Netanyahu's rhetoric needs to be situated in a context. He made his statement at a time when international sympathy for the Palestinians was growing along with criticism of Israel over its ever-expanding settlements and its stalling tactics in negotiations. His majority in the Knesset also rested on a shaky sixty-one-vote majority. Presenting Palestinians as Nazis, Netanyahu probably felt, might draw a bit more support from his center-right allies and from vacillators in his own party: *Likud.* Making provocative statements and then retracting them is the tactic employed by every demagogue. And if it isn't him making the statement, then it is his advisors. Netanyahu's ultra–right wing deputy foreign minister, Tzipi Hotovely, noted around the same time that she hoped the Israeli flag would soon be flying over the holy sites of Jerusalem—not exactly words to inspire feelings of cooperation. Supposedly under pressure from her boss, however, she too immediately qualified her words (with yet another wink): they apparently constituted a personal opinion rather than an expression of policy.

Seemingly having lost the moral high-ground, sensing his growing isolation, Netanyahu's rhetoric must have seemed a safe bet. Soon he would shuffle his cabinet by entering into a "unity coalition" with the right-wing extremist party Yisrael Beiteinu making its leader Avigdor Liebermann his secretary of defense, and thereby gaining a solid sixty-six-vote majority in the Knesset (*New York Times*, 25 May 2016). Netanyahu was trying to please his future extremist allies. His rhetoric justifies them in circling the wagons and in their exaggerated commitments to nationalism, militarism, and imperialism in the present. His words imply that negotiations with this kind of enemy are worthless—and, in fact, thoughts of "appeasement" arise.

Whether any of this is meaningful in its own terms is irrelevant. Demagogic rhetoric is not meant to engage critics in a discourse. It rests on exigency alone. Yet, such rhetoric also reflects a psychological dynamic at work. That Palestinians had virtually nothing to do with the Holocaust leaves intact the lingering prejudice *that they would have participated* if only they had been given the chance. Ironically, this is the very argument that was employed by defenders of the *Protocols of Zion* when confronted with its fabrication and empirical falsehoods during a sensational trial in Bern, Switzerland, in 1934.[2] Exaggeration, paranoia, and projection underpin not just anti-Semitism but bigotry and the authoritarian style. The irony is bitter: Netanyahu was actually promoting the very sort of political hysteria employed by the totalitarian regime from which Jews suffered so terribly. The tragedy is that Israel is mimicking its persecutors—and snickering as its values erode. That is worth thinking about as new demagogues speak their lies and try to avoid the dustbin of history.

11

Garbage People

In 2011 I was in Cairo with a delegation from US Academics for Peace. Trite as it sounds, we had a fascinating taxi driver. He was a Coptic Christian who applauded the overthrow of President Hosni Mubarak and his coterie. He accompanied us to the huge and thrilling demonstrations of May 1 in Tahrir Square, birthplace of the democratic revolution, and he talked with us about events that accompanied the mass uprisings: the fear of military rule, the rise in crime, the lack of tourists, the collapse of social services, and—most strikingly—the indifference of the omnipresent police to assaults upon Christians and other minorities. When we were alone, our driver made me a proposal. He said that if I promised not to mention his name, he would take my wife and me on a little excursion to a neighborhood known as "the garbage village."

Cairo is the largest city in Africa and it's filthy. The banks of its many brooks, the crevices of its many streets, and even its richer sections are littered with refuse. Our driver noted that latter fact as we approached our destination. Large banners with the faces of nine young men killed in assaults by Muslim mobs (which any number of imams later condemned) were hanging between buildings. We would soon see the remarkable churches that were funded from tiny donations and that hold ten thousand parishioners. These places of worship had been constructed in the caverns of mountain and adorned with immense carvings of Biblical scenes. What they overlook, however, is an insult to God—and humanity.

Poverty knows no particular faith: it works on Christians and Muslims alike. Egypt is a nation in which 70 percent of its citizens are "poor" and 10 percent are "destitute." But the degree of misery experienced in the garbage village is something special. Many such impoverished garbage towns exist in Egypt (and elsewhere in the world as well), and the largest has forty thousand residents. The overwhelming majority are Coptic Christians who originally raised pigs that fed on the garbage. Spurred by a wave of fanaticism and fear of swine flu, however, three hundred thousand animals were slaughtered in 2009—though no case of the disease was ever documented. Only a few half-starved goats now wander about the garbage village that is basically composed of ramshackle houses, cheerless cafés, empty shops, and a few dreary public buildings. Everyday life is powered by refuse. With the privatizing of sanitation services, indeed, garbage freely adapts to the commodity form. It is carried into town on broken-down trucks and overflowing carts dragged by emaciated donkeys. The garbage is then taken to buildings in which it is subdivided for any number of overstuffed apartments where entire families sort it, bind it, and prepare it to be sold to huge recycling plants. The product is then recycled and more garbage is created in what amounts to a circular process.

Garbage blurs the line between public and private space. It sets the stage on which individuals play out their lives. Its stink fills the air that the garbage people breathe. It lures the swarming flies whose numbers are so great that they blur the vision. It carries the germs that produce the countless diseases. It intensifies the already searing heat that often reaches 110 and sparks fires here and there. Grungy children play in the garbage. Wives cook food, hang out clothes on crumbling balconies, and give birth in the garbage. Men work in the garbage, smoke their hookahs in the garbage, and lose their teeth in the garbage. Old people with vapid eyes cough loud and long as they make their way down the streets where the garbage is stacked high on the sidewalks. These are people with hollow eyes waiting to die amid the vermin and the stench and the heat and the dust.

But is the garbage village really such an affront to human dignity? Democratic revolution has been crushed: a new dictatorship is being built, unemployment is rampant, the jails are bursting with inmates, and the Muslim Brotherhood as well as groups associated with al-Qaeda and ISIS are waging guerrilla war against the state. Many realists will say, albeit sadly, that there are issues more important that the plight of forty thousand garbage people. Egyptian traditionalists will insist that outrage is a product of alien attitudes and that such poverty is "normal" in the region. All its cities have slums and ghettoes. Sophisticated travelers often note that worse (*sic!*) horrors can be found in the hellholes of Brazil, China, Congo, Darfur, India, Indonesia, or God knows where. An excuse always exists to avoid redressing the inexcusable—and it doesn't take much to shift the viewer's gaze from the matter at hand. My memory of our driver and the garbage people has already grown dim. The only reminder is the lingering chill of the words written so long ago by Bertolt Brecht that bring *The Threepenny Opera* to a close:

> And there are some who live in darkness
> And there are others who live in light
> And one sees those in the light
> Those in the darkness disappear.

12

Hidden Nations, Enduring Crimes

Tbilisi looks much like Turin or many other beautiful cities in Northern Italy. Only it is poorer—much poorer. The capital of Georgia sits amid hills, lush valleys, and flowing rivers. Old reconstructed houses are lodged into bare mountains. New commercial avenues mix with hideous remnants of Soviet architecture and marvelous Byzantine churches, some dating from the fourth century, along with other visible symbols and signs of the feudal past. Still emerging from the shadow of communism, and a shabby war with its Russian neighbor, Tbilisi hosted a remarkable conference in 2010—Hidden Nations, Enduring Crimes: The North Caucasus between Past and Future—that dealt with the nineteenth-century genocide waged by Imperial Russia against Circassians and other peoples of the Caucasus. Working-class activists mixed with businessmen and politicians entered into intelligent and often heated debate with students and academics. The impressive list of participants included André Glucksmann, the late human rights activist and controversial philosopher; scholars of the region like Robert Chenciner of Oxford University, an expert on Dagestan and Kaitag embroideries; and Lord Frank Judd of Great Britain. Former chair of the Refugee Committee, and Rapporteur to the Political Affairs Committee on the Conflict in Chechnya for the Council of Europe, Lord Judd gave an impassioned plenary speech about the repression and the regional saber-rattling of the Russian Federation—and the need for the world community to demand accountability. This was among the dominant themes of the conference. There was none of the one-upmanship that usually runs rampant at mainstream academic meetings—perhaps because something was at stake, namely, recognizing the forgotten genocide suffered by a hidden nation and dealing with its quest for a national identity.

Genocide is a difficult legal concept to prove, though age-old reports prepared for the czars might provide documentation of what took place in the Caucasus in 1847. Clarity about genocidal acts involving mass murders, deportations, and attempts at ethnocide would build solidarity among and with the Circassian community. Such policies constitute a tradition of repression that extends from long-forgotten nineteenth-century czars to Stalin and current conflicts between Russia and Chechnya that have cost well over two hundred thousand lives. Fine conference papers documented the atrocities perpetrated against the indigenous peoples of the Caucasus. To the extent that they were listening, moreover, Russian leaders received a wakeup call to reflect upon their imperialist ambitions and provide their formal federation with democratic substance.

The Caucasus is lodged between the Black and the Caspian Seas and it stretches from Azerbaijan in the south over Georgia to Chechnya and North Ossetia. Many of its inhabitants suffered terribly at the hands of Stalin. Everyone knows about the Holocaust, but the victims of the Gulag have still not received their due. Few outside the Caucasus have ever heard of many Circassians, though exile communities exist in Israel, Jordan, Syria, Turkey, and the Western democratic nations. The genocide of the Circassians, and other indigenous peoples of the Caucasus, has been ignored as surely as that inflicted on Native Americans in the United States and the indigenous peoples of Latin America by Spain. Lidia Luposova—twice nominated for the Nobel Peace Prize—shocked the conference with a photo exhibition of Chechens (mostly children) victimized by Russian military and security forces. The acknowledged leader of the Grozny branch of Memorial, the courageous Russian human rights organization, Ms. Luposova risked her life (once again) to take those photos and to publicize them. Hidden crimes like those depicted by her exhibition are not part of the public discourse—and learning about them led me to think, once again, about our lack of a cosmopolitan sensibility and how little we know (or care) about the larger world outside our own town or country.

Ignorance has political implications. Little can be done about the past, but much can be done about the present and the future. Few waste much time thinking about the war waged against Chechnya by Russia, especially since it has been justified as a war against terror. Russia still insists that "foreign extremists" (Islamic radicals) are the cause of all their problems. The repression has been ruthless. Not only are supposedly surgical missile strikes employed but (as speaker after speaker insisted) violence is targeting the entire civil society of Chechnya: its economic infrastructure, its legal system with its politically compromised judges and lawyers, its media and its intellectuals. There is no evidence that foreign elements like al-Qaeda have entered the fray or that a Russian state weakened by internal saboteurs is the cause of rebellion. But they are part of the propaganda offensive directed against various Caucasian movements seeking greater autonomy or self-determination. The new Russia is undergoing an authoritarian makeover that relies on paranoid fears of implosion and Western imperialist designs. In fact, however, Russian security forces have sponsored many of the terrorist attacks undertaken by Chechen criminals and terrorists. The new Russia apparently fears Chechnya's demands for autonomy will serve as a precedent for other states—and for good reason.

There is nothing new about the appeal of nationalism within the region. The great debates over national self-determination at the start of the twentieth century between Lenin, Rosa Luxemburg, Otto Bauer, and others revolved around burgeoning developments in the Russian and Austro-Hungarian empires rather than in Africa, Asia, or Latin America. There are today still deep-seated longings to affirm cultural identities that have been under attack for two centuries. Resistance is growing in Azerbaijan, Kazakhstan, Kyrgyzstan, Tajikistan, Turkmenistan, Uzbekistan, and other nations. The protest is mostly Islamic, partly secular, often inchoate and confused. Bloody terrorist actions have taken place for which innocent citizens suffer and for which subaltern organizations and hegemonic forces bear mutual responsibility. Tensions between many of the different ethnic communities still fester. Whether an independent Caucasus is feasible remains (at best) a debatable proposition. But then the same can be said about other communities longing for nationhood. Even long-standing states, whose national unity was once taken for granted, are now imperiled by civil war and potential disintegration. Syria is a case in point and perhaps the following interview will provide some insight into the problems of leadership and sovereignty.

13

Visiting Assad

READER *SUPPORTED NEWS*: Tell me something about your encounter with Bashar al-Assad? What did you think of him? How did he impress you?

STEPHEN ERIC BRONNER: In 2005, I spent about two hours with President Assad, and then another hour or so with his wife, Asma, as part of a delegation sponsored by US Academics for Peace that included James Jennings, the president of Conscience International, Lawrence Davidson, Bianca Jagger, and a number of other activists. A report of that meeting appears in *Peace Out of Reach: Middle Eastern Travels and the Search for Reconciliation* (2007). I found Assad cold and stiff in his demeanor but articulate, intelligent, and exceptionally well informed. I saw him then as an authoritarian with reformist sensibilities. He spoke vaguely about transitioning to a parliamentary democracy and stepping down. But we didn't take these words very seriously. Most politicians cling to power as long as possible—especially dictators.

RSN: When Bashar al-Assad came to power twelve years ago, the international community thought he would be the person to change Syria, and Bashar al-Assad did express his willingness to change. But it seems it did not lead in the right direction. Why wasn't he able to reform Syria? What are the biggest obstacles?

SEB: Media pundits initially suggested that Bashar al-Assad was cut from very different cloth than his father. Hafiz al-Assad was crude in demeanor and provincial in outlook. He had a military background and lacked any direct experience with democracy. In the West, many considered him little more than a ruthless Soviet stooge. Hafiz was actually already a Cold War relic when he died in 2000. Hopes grew when Bashar succeeded him. He had been educated in England, studied ophthalmology, and—it was assumed—internalized elements of the liberal spirit. His beautiful and highly educated wife, Asma (whose Sunni family comes from Homs), was born and studied finance also in England. Both appeared cultured and intellectual. They were also photogenic—a Middle Eastern version of John and Jackie Kennedy. This indeed was the couple that the Assads self-consciously sought to emulate and the popular media endeavored to present them that way, especially as the civil war took its toll and the legitimacy of Syria's first couple began to falter. In any event, many believed that Bashar was not driven by political ambition. He may have risen in the military and played a role in the Syrian invasion of Lebanon in 1998, but he was originally not meant for politics and he came upon the scene only after the death of his brother in an accident. More civilized behavior was undoubtedly expected of him; thus, the more intense the disappointment and the criticism following the atrocities in Homs, Idlib, and elsewhere. But Bashar was still part of the ruling family, the military, and the Alawite community. He fit seamlessly into the power structure. His attempts to modernize Syria called for him to deal with loyalties and conflicts emanating from pre-capitalist and sub-national institutions and traditions associated with clan, tribe, and religion. Navigating such waters is undoubtedly difficult. Nevertheless, ultimately, economic and social progress requires the kind of open society and democratic polity that the secular authoritarian fears.

RSN: Do you think Bashar al-Assad ever tried to introduce meaningful change into Syria? What were the changes? In the early years of his rule, Bashar al-Assad "gave up" his idea of political reform and said economic reform must be first. He tried to established private banks and so on. But in the recent years, Syrian economy became even worse. Why?

SEB: When I was in Syria (and also when I visited Iraq in 2003 just before the American invasion) it appeared that much effort had been spent on education and, at least in the cities, everyday life exhibited a certain cultural (if not political) pluralism: it was possible to see, for example, women in religious garb and others in miniskirts sitting in the same café. Both Bashar al-Assad and his wife expressed the desire to increase the number of computers and the degree of computer literacy. They spoke about privatizing the banks and other industries as well. They also expressed concern with improving health services and the conditions of women. Liberalizing the economy and society, however, always has anti-authoritarian political implications. And, when these become too threatening, the dictator generally retreats into what he knows: repression. Bashar al-Assad introduced a new constitution and often spoke vaguely about changes in the parliament. But meaningful democracy presupposes contested elections, free assembly, free speech, civil rights, and the liberal rule of law. All of these constrain the arbitrary exercise of political power. Wielding authority in that way, however, is precisely what defines the dictator. Politics is always in command and maintaining power is the primary concern—no matter what the cost. Economic determinism simply doesn't work here. Dictatorial regimes breed a culture of corruption and inefficiency. The bureaucratic hierarchy is intertwined with tribal and familial bonds that are made more complex by religious connections. All this undermines the modernizing process that the secular dictator supposedly wishes to introduce. Finally, there is a kind of parochial rigidity—and the prevalence of what various social thinkers have termed an "authoritarian personality" structure—that makes it difficult to deal with the dynamics of an increasingly global society.

RSN: How do you understand the thinking of Bashar al-Assad? Is he unique or not? Does he have as firm a grip on power as his father?

SEB: President Bashar al-Assad, it should be remembered, is a secular authoritarian. He is not really so very different from other dictators in the region. His tradition begins with Kemal Atatürk in Turkey and carries over to Saddam Hussein in Iraq, Nasser and Mubarak in Egypt, and others. All of them were brutal in their methods, though most experts of Middle Eastern affairs assumed that each was also committed to modernizing his nation. All of them justified their dictatorial standing by making reference to the dangers of tribal or ethnic conflict and the prospect of attacks on minorities and religious intolerance by Islamic radicals should they ever fall from power. Hafiz al-Assad ruled Syria for nearly thirty years. He killed more than thirty thousand citizens of Hama alone in quashing the 1982 uprising led by the Islamic Brotherhood. But numbers don't tell the full story. Bashar al-Assad has been ruthless enough. He, too, feared the slippery slope whereby introducing reforms would further fuel mass protest and ever more radical demands. Bashar al-Assad has bombed his own citizenry, unleashed state terror, and fiercely suppressed dissent. The apple does not fall that far from the tree. Most dictators enjoying military superiority and the support of powerful allies would probably have acted no differently than Bashar in the face of widespread yet profoundly fragmented oppositional forces.

RSN: Bashar al-Assad seems to face a very different regional landscape from his father. What are the differences? How did he adjust his foreign policy in the past twelve years to fit in the landscape?

SEB: Syrian foreign policy has been complicated under Bashar al-Assad. He has retained the steadfast support of Russia, which goes back to the time of his father, and he also improved relations dramatically with China. Branded a rogue state and a supporter of terrorism by the United States, Bashar al-Assad tried to stem the spillover of conflict following the overthrow of Saddam Hussein and also temper an always uneasy relationship with Iran. Bound to Hezbollah, which still maintains support for his government, he also expressed intermittent interest in negotiating the status of the Golan Heights with Israel, most recently in 2003. Embarrassment resulting from the death of former prime minister Rafic Hariri of Lebanon in 2005, an event that surely involved his regime, led Assad to withdraw troops from the border and—at least in form—retreat from direct involvement in his neighbors' domestic affairs. There is little doubt that Bashar al-Assad wanted to be a principal mediator in events affecting his region of the world—and perhaps even beyond. Of course, this dream has collapsed. He has now been forced to deal with a world very different from the one in which his father operated. During the reign of Hafiz al-Assad, the Internet and the cell phone did not exist. The world community read about the mass murder of Syrian insurgents but it did not experience them in a visceral fashion. Then, too, the Middle East was not really part of the public consciousness as it is today in the aftermath of 9/11 and now the Arab Spring. Condemnation by world public opinion and the inspired international resistance generated by the Arab Spring did not crystallize against the father as they did against the son.

RSN: Murder in Syria shocks the world. What are the reasons for it? Is it possible that Bashar al-Assad made some real concession? Does Bashar al-Assad still control his army and elites in the revolt now? If Assad lost political power, who do you think would replace him?

SEB: For authoritarian rulers, indeed, the horror that their actions inspire among ordinary people is a secondary concern. Whether Assad is determining the specifics of military policy or not, he is clearly the face of the regime—and there is little reason to doubt that the buck stops with him. His strategy is clear. Assad is counting on the inefficiency of a fractured opposition while the opposition is counting on the defection of troops from Assad's army. Without referring to the matter of foreign intervention, or what might happen should the Syrian conflict spill over into Lebanon or Turkey, the degree to which the opposition is unified is the degree to which it can demand concessions and forge a common destiny. Without solidarity, paramilitary organizations will emerge with conflicting aims and ambitions. Ongoing civil war is not inevitable, but it is likely in the near future. Under these circumstances, it is more important to analyze the forces in conflict (and the structural prerequisites for a more liberal regime in the future) than speculate about which general or party official would replace the current president.

RSN: I read the chapter dealing with Syria and your meeting with President Bashar al-Assad in your book *Peace Out of Reach*. Did you ever meet him again afterward?

SEB: I never met President Assad again. Two hundred and fifty thousand people have died since then, hundreds of thousands more have been wounded, millions have lost their homes, and a refugee crisis of unprecedented dimensions has been unleashed. The country's infrastructure is devastated and the environmental damage is incalculable. With the destabilization of Iraq by the United States, festering religious hatreds coupled with ideologically inspired miscalculations and political rivalries transformed latent possibilities for mass murder, which occurred often enough with Bashar's father, into full-fledged genocide. As things now stand, yet another cease-fire has collapsed and the Syrian National Council is probably in worse disarray than it was a few years back. The rise of ISIS has been accompanied by the rivalry between al-Qaeda and the al-Nusra Front, while Russia has joined Iran in its support of Assad's (Alawite/Shia) regime, and different factions within Saudi Arabia support both Sunni participants in the conflict, ISIS, and its Syrian opposition. Any future regime will not only need to deal with lingering domestic hatreds but also residual paramilitary organizations, minorities that cannot protect themselves, external power brokers, and the lack of a sovereign acceptable to all parties. That is the case whether Syria in its present form continues to exist or whether an Alawite state emerges and the entire country is reconfigured. Genocide is not that difficult to initiate given the proper preconditions—but always much more difficult to stop once underway. That is especially the case in the shadow of war when the train has left the station and starts gathering speed.

14

A Short Report on Violence in the United States

America has been marked by violence from its inception. It has always been bolstered by prejudice, whether with respect to African Americans or Muslims, and in the modern age by the rise of the security state and the unqualified right to bear arms. Today in 2016, of course, fear has gripped the country following the Paris terror attacks and the shootings in San Bernardino, California, that left fourteen people dead and twenty-one wounded. Home-grown terror in the West has its roots in the Middle East where at least four major Islamic extremist groups are fighting one another: ISIS, al-Qaeda, the al-Nusra Front, and the Taliban. Helping one usually means hurting another. Simplistic assessments abound: it is remarkable that those (especially those on the far right) most hysterical about the looming takeover of America by Islam and Sharia law, and most insistent about the importance of bombing ISIS and religion tests for refugees, are those who are most adamant in opposing gun control.

Mass killings in which four or more people lose their lives have become less the exception than the rule: they take place, literally, almost every day. In 2015, 358 cases were reported and, overwhelmingly, the victims were poor people of color (*New York Times*, 23 May 2016). This only makes sense given the multiplication of stress factors that they endure, the frustration that leads to violence, and the underground trade in handguns and arms.[1] Interesting that the entire discussion now centers upon background checks and banning larger (and vastly more expensive) weapons from bazookas to AK-47s. The tables have been turned upon immigrants and the poor: "it is not guns that kill people but people who kill people"—as if the people could be killed without the guns. Vastly more of them are available and vastly more killings take place in the United States than any other Western nation. Mass killings account for 2 percent of the thirty thousand deaths each year from gun violence (*New York Times*, 22 December 2015). With each tragedy, some new idiotic defense of the gun's virtue takes place: Ex-governor Mike Huckabee (R-AR) noted that even individuals on the "no-fly" list should be allowed to purchase guns, while more than one Republican presidential candidate in 2015 noted that had everyday people been armed, the massacres in Newtown and elsewhere would not have taken place.[2] That says it all.

Establishmentarian thinking views the United States as a non-ideological, pragmatic society. Sometimes driven to the left, other times to the right, it always ultimately reaffirms its reliance on what the liberal historian Arthur Schlesinger termed the "vital center." Nothing could be further from the truth. Ideological divisions run deep—very deep—in the United States and organized violence began before 1776. Religious intolerance and genocidal attacks on Native Americans preceded slavery. Abolishing slavery required a civil war, the bloodiest of all our wars, which began with the Confederate attack in 1861 upon the federal government armory at Fort Sumter in South Carolina. Organized terror maintained Jim Crow until people of color gained the vote in 1965 (!). Pitched battles between companies and unions, meanwhile, dotted the twentieth century, while the civil rights and poor people's movements were confronted with violence from their inception. Not only that. There is also the tradition of American imperialist violence that reaches back over Afghanistan and Iraq to El Salvador and Vietnam, Hiroshima and Nagasaki, the Philippines, the Spanish-American War of 1898, and the Monroe Doctrine of 1823 that justified countless U.S. interventions in Latin America. For many, however, this is too abstract. Better to make political violence more "human" by referencing the political assassinations of major figures like King and the Kennedys—and the attempted assassinations of Presidents Gerald Ford and Ronald Reagan—and leave it at that.

Not all of this can be blamed on the political right—but most of it can. Notable is the extent to which the African American community—the principal target of violence—has turned its back on it. Poverty is perhaps less the cause of political extremism than the existential despair of those threatened by modernity.[3] There is a reason why political violence has primarily (if not exclusively) flourished in the more traditional non-urban parts of the country like the South and the Midwest. What Richard Hofstadter once called the "paranoid style" has usually been directed against advocates of cosmopolitan values, democratic reform, and social equality. Liberals, socialists, free thinkers, and—of course—intellectuals, are still seen as enemies of the "real" America: or, better, an imagined community composed of small towns whose citizens are white, straight, virtuous, friendly, and—of course—Christian.

That paranoid style was expressed by the "know-nothings" of the 1840s, the Ku Klux Klan, the "America Firsters" who tended to prefer Hitler to Roosevelt, the partisans of Senator Joseph McCarthy (R-WI) in the aftermath of World War II, as well as the "silent" majority of the 1960s, the "moral" majority of the 1980s, the John Birch Society, and there is more. The paranoid style has been unrelenting in its appeal. It appeared again with the anti-Muslim rhetoric that began after 9/11, simmered during the two terms of President George W. Bush, and then exploded with the right-wing populist upsurge surrounding former Republican vice presidential candidate Governor Sarah Palin (R-AK), who put the nearly assassinated Congresswoman Gabrielle Giffords in the crosshairs of a rifle sight on her Facebook page, a host of successful, reactionary media commentators of whom Glenn Beck and Michael Savage are only the crudest, and—of course—the Tea Party.

Explicit calls for violence by the political mainstream of the Republican Party are rare. More pernicious is their integration not only of the Tea Party but also those even further to the right. The media fascists and their political icons defend their racism in the name of civil liberties, which they always seek to deny their opponents, even as they call for "revolution"—though, naturally, always a revolution that will leave their privileges intact. The approving winks that the Republican leadership casts at those whose resentment against "the system"—or, better, progressives within the system—is impossible to ignore. Their irresponsibility is all the worse given the way in which resentment is now reaching a boiling point.

Centrist Democrats have not been as hard on those legitimating political extremism as they should have been. Reactionaries were undoubtedly emboldened by the mainstream liberal reliance on consensus and compromise that came under withering attack by Occupy Wall Street and the radical left. Blaming these centrist-liberals for the currently decrepit cultural conditions of the nation, however, is as misguided as blaming Social Democrats rather than Nazis for the collapse of the Weimar Republic. Not all those who oppose a more radical commitment to the poor and working people are the same. Only the fringes enthusiastically support violence against doctors performing abortions, against homosexuals, and minorities. Nevertheless, such violence has become a fact of life.

Too often, it goes unreported along with its connection to the ever more acceptable anti-immigrant, racist, and homophobic rhetoric that played such an important role in the Republican primaries of 2016. Neo-fascist ranting about alien, socialist, and communist infiltration has become an acceptable part of political life—and so has paranoia. Especially during the heyday of Occupy Wall Street, death threats mounted against leading left-wing intellectuals like Frances Fox Piven, Cornel West, and others. There is too much talk about "understanding" right-wing rage and too little about appropriate responses. With free speech comes responsibility for what is being said. The influence of words on action is usually indirect, but it is undeniable. That is certainly the case with violence in America. What one reaps is, indeed, what one sows. The real enemy of liberty, civility, and democracy is never hard to find.

Part III

Rebellion American Style

The essays in this section concentrate on the United States and some of the social movements and ideas that gained currency during the Obama years. Certain of them also deal with friends like Bob Fitch and Frances Fox Piven whose thinking infuriated the political mainstream and anticipated what occurred. "Socialism" took on new life in America during these years and congealed into the mass movement supporting the striking presidential campaign of Senator Bernie Sanders (I-VT) to succeed Obama. But that undertaking was itself shaped by Occupy Wall Street and the (often unrecognized) radicalism of Obama's domestic policies. Fear of the Tea Party that conquered the GOP, against conventional wisdom, complemented an assault on the conventional belief that class politics and talk of "socialism" would only turn off American voters. Groups once considered "marginal," fueled by radical and even utopian ideals, confronted what Herbert Marcuse in the 1960s termed the "one-dimensional" society. Thus, the connection became solidified between past and future.

15

Socialism in America

Socialism has had a checkered career in the United States and, historically, its partisans never had a meaningful chance at gaining power. They also never offered a political alternative to the constitutional state in the manner of European socialists, who demanded a republic while operating in a web of monarchies, or Lenin and the Bolsheviks who identified first with decentralized "soviets" and then with their own authoritarian dictatorship of the proletariat. In the United States, however, "socialism" or "social democracy" or "democratic socialism"—whatever the labels employed—privileged economics;[1] its partisans identified with unions and intervention by the existing state into the free market in order to redistribute wealth, and introduce *reforms* to improve the everyday life of working people.

Despite the romantic aura cast over earlier radical movements of the working class, there was actually little talk of revolution other than by certain anarchists and the left-wing faction in the International Workers of the World (IWW), a small syndicalist organization, sectarian Trotskyist sects, and the left wing of the American Communist Party during the "heroic" phase of the Russian Revolution from 1918 to 1921. Or, to put it another way, revolution was demanded only by a small minority of political activists in political organizations that constituted an even smaller minority within the country as a whole. Incapable of attaining political power over the state apparatus, socialists organized from below, served as gadflies for the Democratic Party, and—at their best—participated in the most radical social movements of the moment.

In the Democratic presidential primaries of 2016, Senator Bernie Sanders (I-VT) fused these three strategic options while explicitly identifying himself as a democratic socialist. His campaign mobilized young people and workers garnering $200 million in campaign contributions, virtually all from small donors, pushed mainstream Democrats to the left by limiting the power of the 1 percent through stronger corporate regulation and higher taxes, demanded single-payer healthcare while calling for a variety of reforms beneficial to workers and the poor, and finally rolling back *Citizens United* and the untrammeled use of money in electoral campaigns so that the possibility for a new social movement with political aims might take shape. Interesting is the way in which Sanders' agenda, and what I once termed a class "ideal,"[2] was instantly condemned by its conservative and liberal critics as utopian though virtually every other industrialized democracy already had programs of a similar sort.

But there should be no misunderstanding: his was a reformist program built on the policy framework offered by Barack Obama. His administration had responded to the capitalist economic offensive of the Bush years that resulted in the top one-tenth of 1 percent owning roughly the same as the bottom 90 percent and 58 percent of all new income. In short, the United States had experienced the largest upward shift of income in American history. Wage policies—in the name of the capitalist class (there is no other meaningful way to say it)—had been implemented to deregulate markets, cut corporate taxes, curtail social services, and begin legal proceedings to abolish limits on campaign spending. President Obama responded to this capitalist offensive by demanding subsidies for home owners with mortgages, environmental programs, extension of unemployment benefits, litigation against employers of illegal immigrants, and national health insurance legislation accompanied bailouts of the banks and oversight legislation for the stock market that was described by the *New York Times* (21 May 2010) as constituting "the most sweeping regulatory overhaul since the aftermath of the great depression."

Were these policies "socialist" enough? *Newsweek* certainly thought so: Its headline on February 16, 2009, ran "We are all socialists now!" Senator Sanders obviously generated an even more "socialist" program with an agenda that called for (using an old slogan) "making the bosses pay." But then the real question is whether the Sanders campaign would have been possible without Obama and whether his policy agenda served as the precondition for something else. Powerful elements of the far right intuited this and ultimately their mass constituency galvanized around that perception. "Obamacare" remains under attack for being a "socialist" construct. A phalanx of wildly popular and reactionary radio talk show hosts like Glenn Beck, Rush Limbaugh, and Mark Levin now use "socialism" as a catch-all term to condemn any policy that strengthens the social welfare function of the state. It was the same with the right-wing populist Tea Party.

Anti-welfare state, anti-intellectual, implacably opposed to immigration, and increasingly racist, the new right-wing agenda was predicated on hostility to all proposals for redistributing wealth. Oddly enough, however, conditions existed for the Sanders campaign long before he launched it. Right-wing fears about socialism were not completely unfounded. Polls by Pew, Gallup, and Rasmussen noted that 29 percent of the American public viewed socialism in a positive light and 37 percent considered it superior to capitalism—and the numbers rose to 43 percent among those between eighteen and thirty years of age (*Common Dreams*, 18 May 2010). Nevertheless, the polls noted that the respondents were not necessarily clear about the meaning of terms like "socialism."

Many leftists used "socialism" as an ideal with which to condemn the shortcomings of the Obama administration. And the critique had some legitimacy. Fair criticisms about unnecessary compromises and missed opportunities blended with often overheated claims about being "sold-out" and betrayed. Some left critics suggested that finance reform would not affect the big banks; others insisted that universal health care was impossible without a "single-payer" plan or a "public option," even though that possibility was left open and "Obamacare" insured fourteen million previously uninsured citizens. Still others demanded greater emphasis on job creation and more sympathy for oppressed minorities. The image of FDR was brought into play. But the references were inappropriate: not only did Democrats control both congressional houses, but the subaltern was organized in the 1930s. No wonder that FDR supposedly told the activist union leaders of his time to "make me do it" with respect to the New Deal and, shortly following his election, President Obama uttered the same words. Nevertheless, it was a different world in 2008: unions were much weaker, the communist party had disappeared, and socialists were seemingly irrelevant.

Other than the huge demonstration of one hundred thousand for immigration reform that took place on March 21, 2010, in Washington, D.C., Obama's first term saw barely any organized action from below on any issue concerning foreign or domestic policy (including nationalizing the banks or single-payer health care or foreign policy). And, most importantly, Republicans were unified by party leaders (and the influence of a nascent Tea Party) around an agenda that would oppose every measure introduced by the new administration from budgets to foreign policy to healthcare. They wished to make Obama fail and, in order to do so, they turned themselves into the "party of no!" and an organization that ultimately had no room for its "moderate" wing. Yet the unstated belief existed among many on the left that the moral commitment of the president was in itself sufficient for bringing about qualitative changes and, even while his Affordable Care Act passed the House of Representatives with only one vote to spare, that he wasn't doing "enough"; it's worth noting that Obama won the election in 2008 with 52.7 percent of the vote and that this hardly constituted a mandate. He also was president not of a neutral state apparatus but of a *capitalist democracy* in which the needs of capital could not simply be ignored. It didn't matter. Enthusiastic supporters became disillusioned. They questioned whether voting for him a second time was warranted, while others grudgingly cast their ballot for the lesser evil in the presidential campaign against Mitt Romney in 2012. Obama had raised lofty "socialist" expectations in 2008, and his constituency fervently believed that the nation's first black president would instantly transform the political system, usher in social justice, and redistribute wealth. Even under the best circumstances, this would have been improbable. With the worst economic crisis of modern times, a newly deregulated financial sector, a burst of economic inequality, two catastrophic wars, and a neo-conservative foreign policy, it became impossible. In short, Obama was bound to disappoint.

The new president was not elected to oversee a system in which innumerable factions and lobbies compete for power on an unequal playing field. Capitalist democracy renders employment dependent upon private investment. Labor is subordinate to capital. Workers are forced to rely for their livelihood on the investment decisions of capitalists. In the event that the ruling class feels itself threatened, it can withhold investment or send it abroad. Such is the structural imbalance of class power. Different sectors of capital are, by the same token, often in competition and this enables subaltern groups to intervene in the process. Reform is thereby built into the system, but always within the *existing imbalance of power* that marks capitalist democracy at any given historical moment. No progressive politician—"socialist" or not—can avoid this reality, whether it is a matter of bailing out banks, health care, immigration, or support for the auto industry. But this capitalist reality was never properly articulated during the euphoria of 2008 and even amid the spontaneous eruption of Occupy Wall Street in 2011. The general belief grew: Obama should have done more, he should have done it better, and he should have done it sooner.

Criticisms of this sort are par for the course. Inadequacy lies in the nature of reform. None is ever good enough, it can always be done better, and it always takes too long. Communists expressed the same complaints about social democratic policy in the 1920s, and even during the Popular

Front of the 1930s, while socialists directed them against liberals in the aftermath of World War II. The brief window of opportunity that existed after Obama's election victory in 2008 for dealing with the banks was probably not fully exploited. He may have been too timid in confronting Republicans, and he certainly did not use the bully pulpit of the presidency to maximum effect. While much of the left condemned him as a sellout, however, conservatives and partisans of the ultra-right insisted that he was a communist or a socialist. Claiming that most Americans don't understand the meaning of these political terms is a bit too self-serving: American leftists are not all that clear about them either and often employ them abstractly without reference to existing political circumstances.

Obama was never as radical as many initially assumed and he never identified as a socialist of any sort. But he was no more or less opportunistic than was FDR, Willy Brandt, or a host of other leading postwar socialists. Less clear is why left-wing activists and intellectuals in the United States never treated him that way. His administration engaged in the largest government intervention in American history involving bailouts of the auto industry and the banks, health care, and an invigoration of the welfare state, as well as a cosmopolitan cultural agenda that supported a woman's right to choose, gay rights and gay marriage, multiculturalism, secular education, new directions in foreign policy, and the need to confront climate change.

Preserving a doctrinaire understanding of socialism renders it politically irrelevant. Better to highlight the "socialist" elements of existing proposals that seek to regulate capital and redistribute wealth. Socialism evolves, and articulating criteria for judging policy is part of the challenge facing its contemporary supporters. Criticism of Bernie Sanders and his inability to contest the "system" could also be heard in some quarters. But this all usually occurs at the margins. Commitment to principles should not excuse refusing to engage what exists. Socialism is ultimately an ongoing practical project rather than (as Marx warned against) a model program or a prefabricated ideal. It is a matter of adapting socialism to meet new conditions—not the other way around—while forming a critical tradition from the theory and practice of those who realized that.

16

On Paul Robeson

Holding this talk is a privilege for me—and I would like to thank Edward Ramsamy for making it possible and setting the stage for what will now become a yearly lecture honoring the memory of Paul Robeson. Speaking to you now is also special for me because years ago I lived on Witherspoon Street in Princeton, near where the church stood in which Robeson's father served as pastor, and in the city where Paul was born in 1898. I also appeared on a radio program years ago with his son, Paul Robeson Jr.—or Robby. But there is something else. It is poignant and disappointing, and it deserves mention. I've been at Rutgers University now for forty years. Buildings, centers, and rooms have been named after Robeson. Nevertheless, I believe, the appropriate recognition for Paul Robeson has been lacking—even in the black community: he has indeed become a symbol, but one that has been domesticated and stripped of politics.

Paul Robeson may have received his law degree from Columbia University in 1923, but his name is indelibly linked with Rutgers. A member of its class of 1919, if he is not this university's favorite son—then he should be. There is no other graduate who exhibited such a variety of talents. It was here at Rutgers that Robeson received letters in basketball, track, and football, where he became an All-American, where he deepened his knowledge of literature and theater, where he sang, where he was named valedictorian of his class—and where he read the newspapers that reported on lynching, trumped-up trials for Southern blacks, rank forms of everyday discrimination, the Russian Revolution and the subsequent uprisings in Europe, the red scare of 1919 in the United States, the rise of fascism, anti-imperialist rebellions, Stalinism, the Spanish Civil War, and the anti-fascist Popular Front. Robeson was a witness and a rebel to this flurry of events.

A word about the elephant in the room: many grow uncomfortable when Robeson's communist sympathies are brought to light; many avoid talking about them: that is certainly the case on this campus. Whether technically in the communist party or not, however, Robeson was indeed a communist. He was naive regarding the utopian hopes raised by Soviet industrialization, he misjudged the role of the Soviet Union during the Spanish Civil War and the Popular Front, and his vanity was surely tickled by being awarded the Stalin Prize. He privileged the tactics and uncritically embraced the myth surrounding Communism as if the Soviet Union were still revolutionary and the locus of freedom. But then Robeson was not alone. Sympathizers and those who made excuses for Stalin's show trials, disastrous political misjudgments, brutality, and perversion of Marxism were everywhere. But it is worth asking why so many leading black intellectuals joined the communist party—even if most quit later. The list includes: W. E. B. Du Bois, Charles Padmore, Richard Wright, and Ralph Ellison.

No one has ever accused me of being a shill for international communism. But there is context for the decisions made by Robeson and his comrades. As fascism became ever more of a threat in Europe, and the KKK functioned as a mass-based organization in the United States, Stalin's Communist International experienced a tremendous growth in membership during the 1930s—also known as "the red decade." Soviet industrialization and the apparent successes of the first five-year plan amazed the world. No other movement so consistently supported strikes or radical economic or social reforms to combat the Great Depression of 1929. Only the Soviet Union was ready to send guns and international brigades (whose American variant was known as the Abraham Lincoln Brigades) to defend the Spanish Republic from the fascist forces of General Franco. Even more to the point for Robeson and his friends, no other American political organization was as engaged with the struggle of Southern blacks from the time of the Scottsboro trial to the early days of the civil rights movement. Republicans were traditionalists while Democrats pragmatically accepted racism and segregation as the price for maintaining their Southern base and a bargaining chip for guaranteeing Southern support for the New Deal. In short, there was a vacuum when it came to combatting racism in the United States—and, for better or worse, the communists filled it.

Communist views on race perhaps weren't as sophisticated as those offered by Trotskyist intellectuals like C. L. R. James: During the 1930s, however, the American Communist Party was aligned to a powerful world movement; it was a force rather than a sect and, in contrast to establishmentarian parties, at least it had a "line." Communists were rigid and ruthless but also brave and deeply committed. Especially when far from the centers of power, they often exhibited a genuine generosity and sympathy to the oppressed. Robeson and many of his friends recognized the attempts by communist organizations to balance a historical concern for black identity with the current ideological demands of anti-imperialist and broader class struggles.

Robeson achieved great fame among his contemporaries—and it extended beyond politics. He was an artist in a number of different fields. All his achievements, however, were infected by the racism that his good friend, the great scholar and activist W. E. B. Du Bois, called the "cancer" of the American polity. Robeson saw that disease strengthened by growing intolerance and provincialism. Aside from the discrimination he experienced in the minutiae of everyday life, Robeson was often jeered during speeches and concerts, targeted by right-wing demonstrations, vilified later by McCarthyism, and blacklisted while being kept a prisoner in his own land. It is not as if consensus existed for his support of anti-lynching laws, civil liberties, the Spanish Republic, or the Soviet Union even during the Popular Front. But then, not only was he a communist—he was also a black communist. The kind of bigotry faced by Paul Robeson today seems almost anachronistic—I say almost.

With the killing by police of unarmed African Americans becoming a daily occurrence, and the publicity surrounding the riots in Ferguson Missouri that rocked the United States in 2015, along with the emergence of movements such as Black Lives Matter, it would seem that both the need and the possibility exists for a more robust historical and political discussion of bigotry. A federal investigation of race relations in Ferguson showed that between 2013 and 2015 blacks accounted for 93 percent of all arrests, 90 percent of traffic tickets, and 95 percent of discretionary arrests like jaywalking (*New York Times*, 4 March 2015). The killings there are not aberrations but rather part of a pattern: Anywhere from one to three supposedly "justifiable homicides" by police shootings—overwhelmingly targeting people of color—take place every day all over America. Long-standing tensions exist between the police and those ghettos and neighborhoods in which minorities predominate.

As I suggested in *The Bigot* (Yale University Press 2014), however, beginning a meaningful discussion about race is inhibited by the ways in which prejudice is adapted to the acceptable conventions of our society. Bigotry is camouflaged as the bigot turns it into justifications for public policy. Legislation to curtail voting is legitimated by a concern with preventing "fraud," cuts in the welfare state by the need to foster a sense of concern with personal responsibility, opposition to gay marriage and abortion by the desire to defend tradition and out of religious considerations. The bigot today hides his ulterior purposes. For all that, the victims of discrimination remain the same: people of color, women, gays, and the "poor" or working class that, together, constitute the majority of society. Robeson's old concern with linking black identity to broader battles against poverty and class struggle remains our project.

Unfortunately, however, popular understandings of the bigot remain anchored in an earlier time. His critics tend to highlight the personal rather than the political, crude language, and sensational acts rather than mundane legislation and complicated policy decisions. Words wound but the truth is that policies wound even more. Everyday citizens grow incensed when some commentator lets slip a racist or politically incorrect phrase. But they are far more tolerant when faced with policies that blatantly target and disadvantage the bigot's usual victims. After all, reasonable people can disagree about this or that policy as it applies to gays, people of color, and the poor. But then ethical suspicions must arise when an entire agenda is involved. No conservative political organization today has majority support from women, the gay community, people of color, the working poor, or the unemployed. There must be a reason. Critics of prejudice should begin placing a bit less emphasis on what the bigot says or "really" feels than what he actually does.

And what of Robeson? He was just what the bigot hated most. A handsome and angry black man, erudite and articulate, accomplished and poised. He worked hard, very hard, until not long before his death in 1976. He finished law school while playing in the NFL. He was the first African American star of a major motion picture, *The Emperor Jones* (1933), redefined Othello, and became a major interpreter of Eugene O'Neill. Later, when denied a passport, Robeson argued his own case before the Supreme Court. He called for integrating unions, supported strike actions, and raised awareness about the terrible plight of Australian aborigines. He was an archaeologist of African traditions and, as a popular writer and publicist, a unique representative of the Harlem Renaissance. And then, of course—there is his signature song "Old Man River"—a song of freedom and rebellion that Hollywood used to portray the African American's acceptance of his miserable fate.

Paul Robeson was arguably the greatest African American public intellectual—among the greatest ever produced by the United States—during the first half of the twentieth century. He was a politically engaged artist who evidenced a concern for his roots and a cosmopolitan sensibility. He made his political mistakes—and they were often grave. But in a dangerous political climate, at least, he dared to make them. For young people seeking a celebrity role model who is something more than a celebrity, there is no place better to look than to Paul Robeson.

17

Remembering Fitch

Recollections of a Solitary Syndicalist

Bob Fitch died on March 4, 2011, at the age of seventy-two. I first met him in Berkeley during the early 1970s and then, until shortly before his death, we continued to meet every month or two at Pete's Tavern on 18th Street in Manhattan's Gramercy Park. It remains one of the oldest restaurants in New York City. Intellectuals and political people used to gather there, and it was the place where O. Henry supposedly wrote his great short story "The Gift of the Magi" (1905). Pete's Tavern was always noisy, packed with people, and the food was not great. But it was near Fitch's tiny apartment on 17th Street and it reminded us of an admirable past. I can barely remember a conversation with him that did not involve the radical literary or political heritage of times past. And it was almost as if he had read too much. Historical insights, stories, bristling ideas, facts upon facts, and pregnant theories played off one another in his remarkably fertile mind. How often, after a debate on some obscure issue or another, Fitch would call the next day to say that he had checked it out—and found a citation that clarified the matter (and, usually, validated his position). He was a terrific interlocutor: one walked away from a discussion with him smarter—and more intellectually honest—than before.

Fitch showed little patience for the fashions associated with the 1960s and its aftermath: authoritarian Marxism, identity politics, populism, spiritualism, or what much later would become known as the "politics of meaning." He was a person of great intellectual depth. Fitch studied the culture of classical Greece (like everything else) on his own. His political outlook fused the communitarian ideals of Rousseau, the ethical rationalism of Kant, the critical political economy of Marx, and a vision of unions as the expression of working-class solidarity that derived from Durkheim and

Eugene V. Debs of the Industrial Workers of the World (IWW). But Fitch the theorist was also concerned with practice. He first joined a union when he was fifteen and then, after a stint in military intelligence while in the air force, he wound up in Berkeley. Radicalized by the 1960s, for a time, Fitch became something of a Maoist. He helped create the Revolutionary Union that, under the stewardship of Bob Avakian, turned into the Revolutionary Communist Party. But Fitch lacked the sorry megalomania of so many revolutionary sectarian "leaders." He was never intoxicated by violence. A trip to Eastern Europe soured him on communism and vanguard politics. Fitch was also skeptical of third world populism: *Ghana: End of an Illusion* (1966) that he coauthored with his wife at the time, Mary Oppenheimer, provides a sobering analysis of the overthrow of Kwame Nkrumah.

Fitch worked at Local 802 of the American Federation of Musicians from 1989 through 1990. Our common friend, Manny Ness, recounted how he organized many shops for the union and was considered a model organizer. Fitch was then hired by CWA Local 1180, a union representing New York City public employees, to develop a plan for rebuilding New York's eroding manufacturing base. His research would serve him well and, in the process, Fitch became aware of corruption in the union ranks. He refused to turn a blind eye—and his public estrangement from organized labor began. To the day he died, however, Fitch was respected by many leading union officials and, in private, some of them continued to ask his advice on union revitalization.

While in Berkeley, along with David Horowitz and David Collier (both of whom later turned to the far right), Fitch served as an editor of the iconic New Left magazine *Ramparts*, and he later helped found *Socialist Revolution*. So, now, he turned back to journalism. He became one of the finest essayists of the 1960s generation. Many of his articles and editorials dealt with the nitty-gritty of urban politics. Others were concerned with crisis theory and the contradictions plaguing American capitalism. "Who Rules the Corporations?" (1970), also written with Mary Oppenheimer, illuminated the empirical organizations, workings, and interests generated by the existing accumulation process and what Marx called the "political economy of capital." Fitch was intent upon finding the great within the small: it was perhaps the fundamental theme that ran through his work.

Empirical inquiry was intended, according to Fitch, to illuminate the larger structure and spur indignation against it. And the wealth of his empirical knowledge was amazing. Nowhere does this become more apparent than in the collusion of finance, insurance, and real estate—or what he termed

"FIRE"—that resulted in the loss of manufacturing jobs in cities and their transformation into metropolitan playgrounds for the wealthy at the expense of working people. *The Assassination of New York* (1996) exposed the forces of capital working hand in hand with city officials in both parties—when it came to subsidies or housing or jobs—and it created a sensation. Many urban activists and students of city life still consider it a classic. But Fitch received only criticism from liberals for its attack on the Democratic Party establishment and, following the coronation of Rudy Giuliani as "America's mayor" in the aftermath of 9/11 (and his disastrous showing in the Republican primaries of 2008), it has largely been forgotten.

The Assassination of New York was based on articles that first appeared in the *Village Voice* and *The Nation*. It seems far removed from the university towns and populist politics that were so much a part of the New Left. But Fitch never fully abandoned Berkeley. His romantic vision of solidarity, or "class consciousness," hinged on popular democracy. Fitch was committed to the empowerment of workers and ordinary communities—and exposing the obstacles that hindered it. Fitch identified with working-class neighborhoods resisting the capitalist-city government and local unions challenging larger ones. He also envisioned these proletarian communities and unions linking up with one another to create a systematic and organic alternative from the bottom up. He looked back to the Knights of Labor and the IWW for inspiration. Fitch was always a syndicalist at heart—and that got him into trouble.

Solidarity for Sale (2006) was his favorite among the books that he wrote. Known simply as an expose of union corruption and as an unqualified indictment of the labor movement, it was neither one nor the other. Fitch intended to provide a theory of union corruption and his attack was directed less against industrial than craft unions. The problem was that the cavalcade of stories and statistics in his sprawling book obscured the underdeveloped theory and smothered the nuance. Fitch knew that unions were important organizational forms for resisting capitalist exploitation and that they remain relevant. He admired the large and bureaucratically efficient European unions for their relative lack of corruption and the benefits that they provided workers. Fitch believed that the fragmentation of American unions helps explain the widest inequality of income and the most debilitated welfare state in the Western world. For him, then, the issue was not unions per se but the way in which they are organized in our country or, better, what European labor activists still call "the American disease."

Fitch knew that capital has the upper hand in capitalist democracy. He noted the debilitating impact upon labor of weak laws, employer criminality, and de-industrialization. But he refused to cast unions simply as victims trampled by external forces beyond their control—and that made him special. Fitch insisted that the American union movement was complicit in the erosion of its membership and its power. He believed that particular forms of union organization are capable of strengthening or weakening the ability of workers to confront capital. Fitch despaired over a situation reminiscent of feudalism in which twenty thousand semi-autonomous craft unions fragment the workforce while low-level officials depend upon the favors of higher-ups to control jobs within their local jurisdiction. Fragmentation creates problems of enforcement that lead local union leaders into the arms of the mob thereby further eroding their accountability and strengthening their willingness to sell out their membership. Stagnation and ideological drift result—even the most critical reforms lose their appeal.

Ironically, for this syndicalist, the problem was not too much bureaucracy—but too little. What Fitch termed the "fiefdom syndrome" undermines class solidarity and incentives to organize the unorganized even as it fosters the most craven compromises with capital. For him, indeed, the question was not why American unions were weak but why they were once so much stronger. He believed it was due not to the pragmatism and reformism of rival union federations, but in spite of them. Capital was pressured by the state to recognize unions in exchange for non-strike pledges during the two world wars, while business leaders felt threatened by radical organizations like the IWW and the CIO. They had generated alternative models and unrest by the working class thus spurring opportunist action by the AFL. Fitch sought to link these two positions. Maximizing state support for labor calls for a unified union movement, while according to him, only small wildcat unions like those of the Chinese restaurant employees in New York City and their spontaneous strikes provide alternatives to the conservative and divided unionism of our times.

Fitch never squared the circle. He could not translate his critique into a practical stance. But that was not what left him isolated. Even today it's not as if any progressive has a clear idea about how to transform American unions. What the left establishment could not abide, however, was Fitch's seemingly sectarian stance. His structural analysis of unions identified internal attempts to reform them, or the old tactic of "boring from within," with the labor of Sisyphus. No one else stated so openly that it was impossible to dismantle the master's house with the master's tools.

Fitch's estrangement from the establishmentarian labor movement really began with what became a prophetic critique of UNITE and John

Sweeney who in 1995 succeeded the stolid and reactionary Lane Kirkland at the AFL-CIO. Hopes for dramatic change were high among the left establishment but Fitch brought his critical perspective to bear. Old union comrades were appalled, academic technocrats sneered, populists recoiled, and the more prized left-wing publications like the *Village Voice* and *The Nation* no longer had much use for him. *Solidarity for Sale* sealed his fate. A small circle of close friends like Mike Hirsch and Jane La Tour remained steadfast. A few more radical journals like *New Politics* still published Fitch. He joined Democratic Socialists of America. Nevertheless, his outlook remained what it was.

Fitch's name still occasionally comes up in conversations dealing with unions. Looking back, however, I can't think of anyone more isolated than this great Marxist voice of American syndicalism. Fitch knew it, too. But he was never bitter. Generous to a fault, and not just when it came to money, he was one of those rare intellectuals who actually enjoyed seeing another writer receive recognition. Until the last year of his life, Fitch never had a full-time academic job. He ran around frantically teaching various courses as an adjunct at different universities, gave a few talks on the side, made a bit of money from his writing, and scraped by. John Ehrenberg, chair of the Political Science Department at LIU, told me that Fitch's students loved him. And I believe it.

Fitch had a wonderful sense of humor and he was a terrific storyteller. Often I implored him to write a memoir about Berkeley in the 1960s. It might have made him some money (which he sorely needed as he grew older). He seemingly knew everyone from Mario Savio of the Free Speech Movement to Eldridge Cleaver of the Black Panthers to Jerry Rubin of the Yippies and Michael Lerner the future rabbi and editor of *Tikkun*. But Fitch always demurred. And it was not merely a matter of humility. He believed that his old stories belonged in the café. Fitch had bigger things on his mind. He was an intellectual of the old school: wide-ranging in his outlook, always ready to battle over ideas, suspicious of the latest philosophical fashion, ever curious, respectful of genuine scholarship, and proud of his erudition. There are few friends from whom I learned so much. His critical spirit, uncompromising intellectual integrity, and unique voice remain with me. I still remember when he wrote the wonderful lines from "Vetting God's Politics" (*MZine*, 4 November 2006) that perhaps best crystallize his political outlook:

> For modernity, political consciousness begins with disenchantment: the understanding that religion is a form of alienation.

Man makes God, not vice versa. No true political dialogue is possible with people who engage in ventriloquial routines with burning bushes, magic mountains, or enchanted clouds. For those influenced by the Enlightenment the claim of being on God's side is not simply unconvincing. It's a coercive, authoritarian form of discourse. Don't tell me what God says. Tell me what you know. Don't tell me what the Lord did. Tell me why it's good to do!

18

Tea Time

> The ideal of American manhood and culture isn't a lot of cranks sitting around chewing the rag about their Rights and their Wrongs, but a God-fearing, hustling, successful, two-fisted Regular Guy, who belongs to some church with pep and piety to it, who belongs to . . . any one of a score of organizations of good, jolly, kidding, laughing, sweating, upstanding, lend-a-handing Royal Good Fellows, who plays hard and works hard, and whose answer to his critics is a square-toed boot that'll teach the grouches and smart alecks to respect the He-man and get out and root for Uncle Samuel, USA!
>
> —Sinclair Lewis, *Babbitt* (1922)

Republicans and their conservative allies insist that religious dogmatism and racism are anachronisms. But their party still serves as the bastion of anti-gay, anti-immigrant, anti-black, and anti-feminist activism. More than that, the Tea Party has become the nest in which conspiracy theories are being hatched: "birthers" still claim (without a shred of evidence), for example, that President Barack Obama was not born in the United States and thus should have been prevented from becoming president. And that would have been the case were it not for dark forces working behind the scenes; Donald Trump first made his name on the national political stage by pointing to the birther conspiracy and, joined by the pundits of Fox News like Glenn Beck and Sean Hannity, helped create an atmosphere in which, according to a poll by the *New York Times* (29 June 2010), about 60 percent of participants in the Tea Party shared that view.

The disorientation and despair experienced by so much of the Republican mass base became palpable in the primary elections of 2016. President George W. Bush had left them with two failed wars in Iraq and Afghanistan, the bursting of the sub-prime housing bubble, and the crashing of the derivatives market in 2007. Mitt Romney was a dud in 2012 and, in 2008, the electoral defeat of Senator John McCain resulted in the first black president of the United States taking office. Military miscalculation abroad, economic collapse at home, and burning political humiliation fueled the stubborn radicalism and small-minded resentment of what would become the Tea Party. Its success—as against that of Occupy Wall Street—is undeniable. Though there were radical right-wing forerunners like the "Gingrich Revolution," it was the Tea Party that ejected moderate (and even somewhat liberal) voices from the Republican Party and transformed it into a rigid and reactionary organization built in its likeness upon small-minded prejudices, unrealistic policies, anti-government ideology, and deeply retrograde activists.

Coming from non-urban areas mostly in the South and the Midwest, but also from white immigrant enclaves in some big cities, members of the Tea Party have their own forms of moral cognition. They have little use for globalization, the welfare state, new social movements, or the "adversary culture" inherited from the 1960s. Wearing revolutionary garb and tricorn hats, disrupting town meetings devoted to health care and other social issues, bullying progressive congressional representatives, and holding rallies of their own, they constituted a new generation of reactionary activists calling for their own brand of "revolution."

The Tea Party meshed libertarian capitalists preaching the gospel of the free market with right-wing populists intent upon rehabilitating "family values," old-time religion, and a parochial vision of community. Over the last century, for the most part, these trends were diametrically at odds with one another: Libertarians had little use for rabble-rousing bigots, religious fanatics, or the like; while populists hated big business, open markets, and the scientific culture of modernity. Ronald Reagan successfully brought these contradictory trends together. He blended the anti-union and deregulating interests of elites committed to classical principles of the free market with the cultural conservatism and hyper-nationalism of the old "moral" majority and burgeoning religious movements. George W. Bush built on that coalition in his disastrous presidencies. But there was new urgency for an alliance between libertarians and populists following the economic collapse of 2008 and subsequent presidential victory of Barack Obama. Fears of dramatic state intervention into the economy blended with the horror over the symbolic impact of a black president on the images justifying white male privilege that were associated with old television shows like *Father*

Knows Best, Leave It to Beaver, and *Happy Days.* Out of this alliance and these anxieties, indeed, the Tea Party was born in 2009.

The GOP was quick to recognize its importance. Seasoned operatives of the Republican Party were soon offering their advice and leadership. They originally thought the Tea Party might be manipulated—just as traditional German conservatives believed that they could use Hitler and the Nazis for their political purposes. Just as in the past, however, the opposite took place in the present: the tail wound up wagging the dog. There is an old saying: styles make fights. Fox News and a score of feral media demagogues, among whom Glenn Beck and Michael Savage were particularly venal, set the tone, employing bellicosity, lies, and forms of vilification that often crossed the line in order to foster blatant prejudice against traditional victims of discrimination. A kind of "us against them" mentality came to the forefront and no quarter was given.

Evangelicals and far-right groups associated with them and the Tea Party routinely began referring to President Obama as the Anti-Christ and as an imam. The bigot applauded. Advertisements compared him and his family to chimpanzees, portrayed the White House with rows of watermelons on the lawn, and implied that the president is a crack addict. But the problem apparently was not the bigot's friends who supposedly hated blacks: rather it was Obama who clearly hated whites. The new president was presented as the advocate of the (black) welfare cheat, the (Latino) immigrant, the anti-Christian (Arab) terrorist, the supposedly overpaid (lazy and shiftless) union worker, and anti-family (feminist and gay) forces. The Tea Party made it easy for even its poorest members to identify with the (white) business elite whose (seemingly color-blind) policies attacking the bureaucratic welfare state appeared intent upon recreating a patriarchal world of white privilege.

Lingering economic recession, fear of social change and economic reform, and fanatical mobilization (coupled with disillusionment of those expecting yet more radical changes by the Obama administration) brought about the sweeping victory of the far right in the congressional elections of 2010. Mainstream Republicans could no longer claim that the Tea Party was simply nuts. It had become the agent of what might be termed capitalist fundamentalism. This meant highlighting the "invisible hand" of the market and the individual (not the accumulation process and class) as the units of social analysis. The state budget could now be equated with a household budget and everyone would echo the mantra of Margaret Thatcher that there is no society, only individuals and families. The welfare state was condemned (once again) not merely as wasteful—but immoral. Hard work brings rewards. Individuals are responsible for themselves, not others. Lack of ambition and foresight by individuals are the causes of unemployment and poverty. No free rides! Evangelicals know the "truth": no abortions, no condoms, and no gay marriage—women back into the kitchen and gays into the closet.

With the increasing influence of the Tea Party and its national posture, (token) possibilities opened up for ambitious individuals who were neither white nor male and who seemingly represented the less privileged. Women like former Republican vice-presidential candidate Governor Sarah Palin (R-AK) or Congresswoman Michele Bachmann (R-MN) reaffirmed the role of the housewife or the "soccer mom" under economic circumstances in which the single breadwinner had already become an anachronism. A gay couple (two male earners) was trotted out occasionally to congratulate the Tea Party for its libertarian values. Log Cabin Republicans, gay and wealthy, got a good deal of press. There was also the future presidential hopeful Senator Marco Rubio (R-FL), who warned of the immigrant mob threatening to invade from south of the border, while an African American businessman named Herman Cain was applauded for insisting that blacks were "brainwashed" into supporting the Democratic Party—thereby confirming the old bigoted belief that "they" are too stupid to favor egalitarian and redistributive policies on their own.

Supreme Court justice Clarence Thomas appeared as a champion of tough love while his (white) wife was a champion of the Tea Party. Congressman Allen West (R-FL), another black politician, employed his civil liberties to tell liberals "to get the hell out of the United States" and then identified the Democratic Party with the Nazi propaganda machine. This cast of characters, it should be noted, was not simply useful for propagandizing the undecided in 2012: it also reinforced the traditional image held by conservative whites concerning what makes a "real" person of color or a "real" woman. All these Republican supporters of the Tea Party validated the benevolent (and completely delusional) image of a bygone America in which taxes were low, government was small, women were in the kitchen, gays were in the closet, people of color gratefully held menial jobs, and the only important color was white. That there is insecurity with this view becomes evident in the attacks on voting rights that continually appear—most recently in North Carolina where a federal judge upheld legislation that would make it unconstitutional for people to register and vote on the same day, curtail early voting by a week, end pre-registration for young people awaiting their eighteenth birthdays, and prevent counting ballots outside the precincts in which they were cast and—of course—tighten voter registration requirements.

All these changes target poor, working-class, and especially African American constituencies. But then the libertarian economic policies promoted by the Tea Party were intent upon undermining democratic deliberation, diversity, and cosmopolitan ideals. A study released on October 29, 2011, by the Bertelsmann Stiftung showed that the United States had plummeted into the bottom five among the thirty nations comprising the industrial world in "Overall Social Justice Rating," "Overall Poverty Prevention Rating," "Overall Poverty Rate," "Child Poverty," and "Income Inequality." Of course, those most disadvantaged are the usual disadvantaged groups. People of color disproportionately suffer from regressive attempts to shrink the tax base and, subsequently, bankrupt the welfare state. African Americans and Latinos are disproportionately impacted by attempts to demand photo ID, literacy tests, and the like in order to vote. Redistricting and racist zoning regulations recreate segregation, while the uncurbed use of private money in election campaigns is disenfranchising working people and the poor. Privatizing the prison system sharply increased incarceration, especially among minority groups: people of color constitute 70 percent of inmates, nationally, and one in three African American males is currently either awaiting trial, in jail, or on parole. Since convicts cannot vote, hundreds of thousands of primarily African Americans and people of color have been disenfranchised by what has been called the "new Jim Crow."

In 2012, there was hardly a single policy proposal forwarded by the GOP that did not disproportionally disadvantage people of color, women, gays, and working people—and, worse, there was hardly a single major Republican politician willing to publicly challenge the rhetoric or the proposals of the far right and the Tea Party. Thus, the mainstream legitimated the extreme. All candidates for the Republican presidential nomination of 2012 worried about a "disappearing white majority" and they took turns attacking the Civil Rights Act of 1964 and the Voting Rights Act of 1965, "food stamp presidents," and critics of religious dogmatism (as well as the Crusades). The same ideology grew even more intense in the gutter campaigns that marked the 2016 Republican presidential primaries.

White supremacists of varying shades tried to recruit and mix with luminaries of the Republican Party at conferences like that hosted by the American Conservative Union. Fragments of half-baked conspiracy theories ran rampant among grassroots activists in the Tea Party. Obama may look like he is in charge but (especially since he is black) he is "really" being controlled by more powerful interests and organizations like the Bilderberg banking group, the Trilateral Commission, Freemasons, Islamic terrorists, or Jews—or all of them working in concert.

Bigotry has again become a commonplace of political life. It is now so much a part of everyday discourse that most people simply shrug their shoulders. The influence of old myths and stereotypes on action has perhaps been perhaps indirect: but it is palpable. Everyday violence (that mostly still goes unreported) against gays, immigrants, and minorities seems ever more routine. Doctors performing abortions outside the larger cities still do so at their own risk. The virtual obsession of the Tea Party with the right to own firearms (including AK-47s) does not merely express a desire to hunt ducks. Mainstream politicians of the Republican Party again either fell into line or were ostracized. School children massacred, black churchgoers executed, and a host of other atrocities were, of course, condemned by all—but then it is never "guns" that kill people, so far as the NRA and the Tea Party are concerned, only "people" kill people.

Sure: explicit calls for violence against the "system" occur only from the margins. Just as the conservative mainstream helped legitimate the Tea Party, however, the Tea Party has legitimated rhetoric and extremists even further on the right—and, worse, the Republican Party still lacks the courage to take them on. Its toleration of the intolerable thus validates precisely what conservatives and those further on the right wish so insistently to deny: racist violence is alive and well in the United States. One just needs to know where to look.

19

Walking Wall Street

Certain times require a spark: September 17, 2011, was one of those times. What became known as Occupy Wall Street struck the match in Zuccotti Park in downtown Manhattan. Frustrated over the seemingly intractable character of the financial crisis that began in 2007, and the inability of established political organizations to challenge growing economic inequality, American activists and anarchists of a new stripe took up a suggestion from the Canadian magazine *Ad-Buster* to "occupy" the center of New York's financial district and the heart of global capitalism. These activists were not part of some half-crazed mob of fanatics as suggested by Newt Gingrich, Eric Cantor, Bill O'Reilly, and other luminaries of the Tea Party and Fox News. Occupy Wall Street was inspired by the Arab Spring but perhaps even more by the then-nascent street protests in Greece, Italy, and other nations teetering on the brink of financial insolvency. Corporations and banks "too large to fail" were everywhere generating the kind of capitalist offensive predicated on deregulation and tax privileges that was virtually unimaginable a generation ago. Thus, spontaneous actions by activists in Manhattan had a mass audience in waiting as a chain reaction of other occupations began not only in the United States but in nearly one thousand cities worldwide.

The ruling classes did not exactly tremble but they were given something to think about. Occupy Wall Street became the catalyst for any number of new movements dealing with issues that ranged from the "livable wage" to jobs creation and to curtailment of the "prison-industrial complex." It also inspired the explicitly democratic socialist campaign of Senator Bernie Sanders (I-VT) in the Democratic presidential primaries of 2016. Occupy drove the Tea Party from the front pages, shifted the discourse from celebrating the free market to demanding government intervention, and thereby invigorated the left.

Ordinary citizens had been caught between a rock and a hard place: Republicans in the Senate and the House were derailing every initiative proposed by Barack Obama, leading him to offer compromises to make them see reason. But these compromises were mostly unsuccessful. Intent upon obliterating the welfare state, and deregulating the private sector, with many House and Senate leaders like Senator Ted Cruz (R-TX) ready to shut down the government by blocking a new budget, Republicans wouldn't give an inch (and, for many, that is still the case). President Obama's ability to offer a vigorous response was undermined not only by the impact of a burgeoning Tea Party, and the timidity of conservative "blue dog" Democrats, but also by the lack of mobilized mass action from the progressive base.

Even his most stalwart supporters were becoming disillusioned and demoralized. Obama's policies appeared as one long unsuccessful attempt to appease the far right and its agenda. One compromise followed another on health care, the bailouts, energy, and the deficits. Traditional demonstrations in Washington and a few other big cities sponsored by unions and various left-wing coalitions calling for more radical legislation (especially on creating jobs) were sparsely attended. They lacked energy and a purposeful sense of solidarity. Obama's early slogans of "Yes We Can" and "hope" rang increasingly hollow with each report of rising unemployment and upward shifts in the distribution of income and wealth. In short, his administration seemed to have run out of gas.

Occupy Wall Street stepped into the breech. Its slogan "We are the 99%!" highlighted the blatant unfairness of a situation in which, according to the Center on Budget and Policy Priorities (9 September 2009), two-thirds of the nation's total income gains from 2002 to 2007 had flowed to the top 1 percent of U.S. households and, in which, taxation was still outrageously skewed to the rich. Federal bank bailouts showed that dominant economic institutions were not willing to play by the rules that they imposed on everyone else. Dealing with an unemployment rate of above 9 percent appeared far less important to Washington than the insistence of the Tea Party for balanced budgets, further deregulation, and tax cuts for the 1 percent that still controls nearly half of the country's wealth and corporations whose outsourcing was strangling the American working class. Occupy sparked demonstrations and unleashed pent-up energy of thousands upon thousands of ordinary Americans who participated in peaceful marches to City Hall, Times Square, and elsewhere. So, while the self-proclaimed "core" loudly (and often self-indulgently) expressed various utopian ambitions and an assault upon liberal politics and government, the mass base of Occupy loudly called for more government intervention into the economy and the host of policy prescriptions that congealed in the Sanders campaign.

Occupy Wall Street had an anarchist flavor. Banners magically appeared and slogans were coined. Tents were pitched, sleeping bags tossed one next to the other, food was donated, first aid stations were manned, and sanitation facilities were imported. Street performers provided entertainment and music. The style was that of the 1960s. A flurry of practical innovation took place in Zuccotti Park. Political forums spontaneously arose with a host of committees, a general assembly, and unwritten rules of procedure to allow even the most reserved to participate. Dozens of plans made the rounds on the web. Some were naïve and others disturbing. A few people envisioned shutting down the Federal Reserve and ending bailouts. There was also talk about a National Convention on the Fourth of July resting on the election of one man and one woman from each of the 435 existing congressional districts to a general assembly that would then present a list of grievances and demands to all branches of government. The refusal to act on them would supposedly result in recalls of all governmental officials including those on the Supreme Court.[1] These utopians showed no lack of visionary ferment as they sought to coordinate various days of action. Nevertheless, while trumpeting the commitment to participatory democracy, there was no accountability to those on the periphery and, in fact, the core wound up distanced from the actual impact of its own movement.

Occupy Wall Street had its pretensions that were celebrated by a pandering media. The young people in the tents and the sleeping bags, who prepared for an indefinite stay in the park, were deeply disillusioned with representative democracy. All of them considered their movement new—a complete break from the past. But it was really a contemporary expression of traditional left-wing populism that reaches back to the nineteenth century, the "Tent Cities" of the unemployed during the 1930s and—of course—the 1960s. Occupy Wall Street was seen by the core as standing in a direct line with the democratic radicalism of the town meeting and the "horizontal" organization of power associated with the Paris Commune and workers' councils.

That only one factory in Oakland was "occupied," however, is telling. Its anarchist advocates were less concerned with radical traditions than creating a new language, a new consensus, and even a new spirituality that would transcend ideology and "political" conflict. Such pseudo-radicalism (and narcissism) made the core of the movement obsessively fearful of cooptation by progressives still willing to play ball with capital and the political establishment—or, better, the inclinations of their own base. Nevertheless, these radicals were subject to the cunning of history: what they thought they were doing was very different from what they were actually doing.

Occupy Wall Street did not transform politics. But its members accomplished a good deal and foreshadowed what would become mass public protests in Wisconsin and Ferguson, Missouri, and elsewhere, against neo-liberal policies and in support of a $15 per hour minimum and "livable" wage campaign as well as protests against the "prison-industrial complex," police brutality (and murder), and the "new Jim Crow" by new organizations like Black Lives Matter. In short, Occupy Wall Street incited previously repressed public anger against inequality and class politics no less than old-fashioned enlightenment concerns with the liberal rule of law and constraining the arbitrary exercise of power by the state. Thus, ironically, the mass of marchers called for transforming the priorities of the very system whose total abolition the core desired.

Liberal pragmatists and political "pros" sitting on the sidelines had no reason to feel smug: Occupy Wall Street did what they did not. Not only did it energize the base of the Democratic Party, but it raised numerous issues that would become important in the presidential campaign of 2016 ranging from free higher education and student loans to aid for the elderly, animal rights, regressive taxation, and the poisoning of the electoral process by big money. Occupy Wall Street gave all these issues a radical spin. It also provided the impetus, pressure, and practical legitimacy for the new emphasis upon public works and the aggressive jobs-oriented left turn by the Obama administration. Even more important, Occupy Wall Street shifted the national discourse from the celebration of deregulation, the free market, small-minded individualism, and a mean-spirited attack upon the welfare state to a new concern with the economic imbalance of power, solidarity, social equality, and the responsibility of government to its citizens. Unctuous questions about what Occupy "really" accomplished indicated little more than bad faith. While the cynics made their wisecracks from the sidelines, Occupy Wall Street sparked worldwide demonstrations with millions of participants who sought to defend workers' rights by standing up against inequality and unemployment.

Occupy Wall Street disbanded in the winter of 2012, promising to reemerge in the spring. But there was never an exit strategy. Activists envisioned new occupations and there were many plans for workshops in nonviolent resistance. But movements cannot be placed in the deep freeze at onc point in time and then defrosted at another. There was no way to accomplish that task anyway: Occupy Wall Street prided itself on rejecting bureaucracy, leadership, and organizational discipline. New concerns might have been publicized. Occupy Wall Street might have focused upon *Citizens United*, which allows for unlimited financial contributions to political campaigns, or defending abortion clinics in conservative states, or mobilizing against a privatized prison system that has disenfranchised hundreds of thousands of the poor and people of color. But this would all have involved making alliances and working within capitalist democracy. Tempering the whip of the market, controlling capital, and preventing poisoning of the electoral process all call for strengthening the bureaucratic welfare state—not abolishing it.

For the core members of Occupy Wall Street, admittedly, it was all or nothing. They refused to distinguish between potential friends within the liberal establishment and staunch enemies within the Tea Party. The spontaneity and anti-systemic radicalism that initially inspired the movement in 2011 paralyzed it in 2012. Nothing happened in the spring or the summer. Mass demonstrations at the conventions of the two major parties never took place. The phoenix did not rise from the ashes. But Occupy should remind progressives of how spontaneous radicalism and organized progressivism can feed off one another in a productive way. Movements and political parties have different roles to play in the political process and tensions will always exist between them. But the role of the movement is probably more dynamic: it alone can badger the mainstream liberal establishment in the name of issues salient to working people and the poor. Occupy expressed a set of romantic hopes. None of the more radical were fulfilled but change happened anyway. Such was the fascinating dialectic in which Occupy Wall Street was enmeshed and which should define its transformative legacy.

20

Vilifying Frances

Full disclosure: Frances Fox Piven has been a close friend for more than thirty-five years. She has served as president of the American Sociological Association, vice president of the American Political Association, and as a leading figure in more than a dozen other associations. A Distinguished Professor of Political Science and Sociology at the City University of New York Graduate Center, she is among the most prominent progressive activists in the United States. With her late husband, Richard Cloward, she also coauthored two classics of social science, *Regulating the Poor* and *Poor People's Movements*, and has written various other works of inestimable value like *Challenging Authority*. For all that, however, there is something curious about the palpable obsession of right-wing pundits with Frances Fox Piven.

The attack was begun about five years ago by David Horowitz, best known for his association with the spurious "Academic Bill of Rights" and his involvement in organizations like Campus Watch that attempt to monitor supposedly subversive professors. Any number of other right-wing luminaries and media pundits soon jumped on board: most notoriously, Glenn Beck. He depicted her on his once immensely popular Fox News television show as the source for both the collapse of the American economy and the ultraradical ("communist," "socialist," "anarchist," "Marxist," or whatever) policies of the Obama administration. Beck's attack was unrelenting. Other notable progressives were targeted by his conspiratorial mindset as well. Another very old friend, Joel Rogers, professor of law, political science, and sociology at the University of Wisconsin, also a longtime activist, and an expert in public policy with impeccable academic credentials, was condemned as the evil "wizard" secretly plotting the urban energy policy of the Democratic Party from behind the scenes. Nevertheless, there is something special about the treatment accorded Frances Fox Piven.

In "The Weight of the Poor: A Strategy to End Poverty," which appeared in *The Nation* (2 May 1966), Frances and Richard called upon poor people to sign up for welfare benefits. Their aim was to foster conditions that might bring about legislation for a guaranteed income. This article is now seen by right-wing media pundits as having caused the state to expand and the budget to bloat. Not deregulation of the financial industry, not corporate mismanagement, not the irresponsible lending of the banks, not capitalist disinvestment or capital flight, not the real estate bubble, not the shift away from industrial production, not the trillions spent on misguided wars, not the looting of social wealth by a tiny elite, or a host of other structural factors associated with the capitalist production process, but Piven and Cloward's incitement to poor people more than forty-five years ago apparently created the conditions for the financial collapse of 2008. What's more, the policy proscriptions by these celebrated academics, obviously inspired by their nihilism, apparently set the stage for healthcare reform, the bailouts of the banks, and other legislation by President Obama to destroy the capitalist system that elected him to office in favor of a revolution that would introduce socialism or communism.

All of this might seem amusing were it not for the death threats and vile messages that Piven received. There was nothing funny about any of that—though, by mocking the article in the *New York Times* that made these threats public, Mr. Beck apparently disagreed. Frances was eighty-three years old and back then she was already the perfect target for some self-righteous schoolyard bully with an ideological axe to grind. "Shoot them in the head" was a phrase used by Glenn Beck in talking about the measures required for taking care of communists. With Frances, however, other possibilities presented themselves: an intentional push to the ground, a quick blow, might have served the purpose as well as a bullet. Hate speech is becoming acceptable in the United States. Disclaimers of violence by reactionary media pundits come along with a knowing wink to the most rabid of their followers. Free speech is today being used to justify what Herbert Marcuse once termed "repressive tolerance." Of course, the ideological ranting by the political right has practical aims. The attack on Piven was clearly an attempt to intimidate the left. It also sought to deflect attention from the real causes of the current predicament—and progressive proposals to deal with it. Then, too, Piven symbolized much of what was best about the sixties and the institution that reactionaries still consider their most implacable enemy: the academy.

Again, there is something . . . well . . . curious about the supposed (conspiratorial) influence being exerted by a brilliant radical woman who, whatever her fame among progressive activists and students, had little influence on the inner circles of the liberal establishment. No one in the Obama administration—at least to my knowledge—supported Frances in calling for a mass movement of the unemployed. Her article in *The Nation* (17 January 2011) that raised this idea, "Mobilizing the Jobless," set off a new series of attacks by Glenn Beck. He surely saw it as part of the "Cloward-Piven Strategy" that, after making its rounds on the Internet, placed these two activist scholars at the epicenter of every progressive movement of the last half century. With this (ahem!) curious analysis, indeed, Mr. Beck and his friends presented in all seriousness a conspiracy theory so Byzantine, gothic, and lurid that it fits nicely into the paranoid tradition best exemplified by the infamous *Protocols of the Elders of Zion.*

Hatching cracked conspiracy theories and labeling accomplished progressive intellectuals as fanatics has always been among the tactics of the far right in America. What better way to discredit the attack on exploitation and disenfranchisement? But Frances Fox Piven did not run from her record. She did not wish to present herself as some kind of centrist mistakenly portrayed as a liberal. Piven frankly endorsed the need for civil disobedience in response to grievances that the establishment refuses to address; she was always an advocate for reforming the imbalances of power in contemporary society; but most of all, she was a political person who drew the most radical implications from the democratic ideal. Even back in 1965, Piven and Cloward were actually doing little more than helping the unemployed and the poor, the economic victims of our system, to exercise their right to welfare benefits. A similar aim informed their decades-long fight for the "motor-voter" bill that so helped poor and working people exercise their electoral rights. The scholarly work and the political practice of Piven and Cloward wished to empower poor and working people—and thus, translate formal into substantive democracy. That is what the right-wing media establishment still considers a crime.

21

One-Dimensional Man at Fifty

Dedicated to Douglas Kellner

More than fifty years have passed since the publication of Herbert Marcuse's *One-Dimensional Man* (ODM) in 1964. That work shaped the first generation of critical theorists in the United States and, while no longer as popular as it once was, it continues to inspire young left intellectuals. Many from an earlier time first encountered the Frankfurt School through Marcuse's citations of works by his friends and colleagues of the 1930s. Erich Fromm was surely more popular, but few knew of his early connection with the Institute for Social Research. As for the writings of now iconic figures like Theodor Adorno, Walter Benjamin, and Max Horkheimer, they had only begun appearing in English translation during the 1970s. For all practical purposes, ODM introduced critical theory to the United States. An interdisciplinary work, which merged the social sciences with philosophy and aesthetics, ODM offered a revamped version of what Antonio Gramsci originally termed "the philosophy of praxis" and—perhaps most importantly—a new critical pedagogy for a movement out of touch with its intellectual roots. Employing the critical method, it questioned old assumptions and predictions. Marcuse adapted Marxism to a new historical context marked by the New Left and an omnipresent postwar belief in "the American Century." Thus, remaining true to the spirit of ODM calls for developing an immanent critique of its assumptions in order to meet the needs of a new epoch and a new society.

Marcuse's classic was structured around what he called the "closing of the political universe." Middle-class suburban life appeared as the apogee of human progress in the 1950s and early 1960s. Social issues had given way to personal concerns, and Germany was marked by a new self-absorbed attitude that held old partisan commitments in cynical contempt and made it clear to new activists that they should pursue their agendas "without me" (*ohne mich*). The Popular Front and the dramatic confrontations with fascism were a distant memory. They had been reshaped and reinterpreted by the mass media and many of the old participants themselves. Social Democracy had identified with the capitalist West in the aftermath of World War II, happily dispensing with its more radical heritage, while Communism grappled with what Sartre termed "the ghost of Stalin." Both sides in the Cold War seemed obsessed with productivity, instrumental rationality, the domination of nature, and intellectual conformity. Stasis seemed to prevail outside of proxy wars and a certain basic ideological competition. Whatever the differences between blocs, however, it was clear that communism was striving for what capitalism claimed to have realized: an abundance of consumer goods and the achievement of what J. K. Galbraith termed "the affluent society."

Especially in the United States, self-satisfaction girded the belief that structural conflict was a thing of the past. Not that this was the reality: McCarthyism had launched an attack against civil liberties, the burgeoning civil rights movement was battling the KKK, which still controlled much of the South, and ten million people remained poverty-stricken in what Michael Harrington termed "the other America." But these entrenched trends were only background noise so far as the mainstream was concerned. In the United States, class contradictions had vanished and what remained were little more than simple differences in the distribution of income and wealth. The welfare state had become part of the consensus and, where social conflict did take place, it was stripped of ideological purpose and transformed into a problem of "public administration." Thus, Daniel Bell made it fashionable to speak about the "end of ideology" in the early 1960s.

ODM was decidedly unfashionable with its esoteric reliance on critique, utopia, and cultural radicalism. One academic publisher after another rejected Marcuse's manuscript until Beacon Press, mostly known for printing Bibles, took a chance. The title struck a nerve, the book turned into an instant best seller, and the publisher became the home of critical theory. ODM introduced a broad public to the dialectical way of thinking developed by Hegel and the young Marx (more concerned with "alienation" than strictly economic or scientific concerns) that was completely antithetical to the common wisdom and philosophical concerns in the United States. Marcuse argued that class contradictions "objectively" continued to exist in "advanced industrial society"—even if they were not "subjectively" recognized as such. He also claimed that the liberal welfare state was not as benign as its uncritical advocates liked to believe and that it rested on what President Dwight D. Eisenhower admitted was a "military-industrial complex" with imperialist ambitions. ODM loosened the straightjacket of political and philosophical conformism by insisting that freedom was not reducible to increased purchasing power, the wares of the culture industry, or the escapades of an imperialist war machine.

Marcuse's work also confronted the way in which the mainstream analyzed problems and reality. It challenged the operational preoccupations, the robotic language, and the supposedly neutral categories of instrumental rationality and analytic philosophy. Marcuse highlighted the exercise of critical reflection and the aesthetic imagination. He understood genuinely radical thinking as intertwined with the development of a "new sensibility," a concern with happiness, and a critique of what was fast becoming a "totally administered society." Borrowing a phrase from André Breton, who had served as the guiding force of surrealism, ODM embraced the "great refusal" with its rejection of mainstream philosophical assumptions and its desire to contest the "totality."

Critical theory would treat all forms of philosophy as inherently value-laden and marked by the historical circumstances in which they emerged. The self-proclaimed concern with neutrality was nothing more than ideology by another name. Positivism and behaviorism, for example, were bent upon excluding subjective interests from the supposedly analytic (objective and value-free) use of language and instrumental rationality. The point was to highlight the operational value of philosophy. These philosophical outlooks had long been targets of the Frankfurt School and, in keeping with its tradition, Marcuse affirmed the status quo by expelling material interests and existential desires from philosophical inquiry. Their ahistorical character naturalized reality and thus demonstrated an unconscious reification of society.

"Critical" theory had originally been juxtaposed against "traditional" theory when the term was first coined in 1938. The new interdisciplinary approach was explicit in its transformative purpose, its historical character, and its unfinished understanding of freedom. ODM was intent upon opening the closed political universe, highlighting new agents of change, questioning the prevailing consensus, and sparking the imagination of an ideologically dulled yet exploited working class. In the first instance this involved confronting the "culture industry," which, in its quest for profits and the broadest audience possible, tends toward seeking the lowest common denominator for its products. The culture industry thus presents the simple, the clear, the unambiguous, and the tried and true. Unconcerned with critical reflection, let alone radical politics, these cultural commodities are inherently "affirmative" of the status quo. Even cynical and hard-bitten crime dramas, let alone saccharine sitcoms, fulfill this aim by rejecting utopian sentiments and insisting that human nature is deeply corrupt and that the brutal existing order is all that there is or can be. The world is left as it is while street wisdom counsels the individual to adapt and "deal with it." The success of such adaptation facilitates feelings of comfort and security and naturally threatens what Hegel called the "unhappy consciousness," the motor of freedom and negation, which longs for the new and projects an emancipated social order. Triumphant in advanced industrial society instead is the "happy consciousness" that excludes meaningful critique and any prospects for developing a "new sensibility."

ODM reflected the aesthetic impulse of the New Left, if not its musical and cinematic tastes, by castigating affirmative culture and the logic of its production. The integrative power of the culture industry led Marcuse to privilege the role of what were then considered "marginal groups" that had been victims of exploitation and prejudice: women, people of color, young intellectuals, and the colonized. Their marginality to the functioning of the culture industry is precisely, according to Marcuse, what enables them to serve as revolutionary "catalysts" for the working class. The groups are supposedly inspired by a new sensibility that militates against cruelty, patriarchal values, environmental devastation, prejudice, exploitation, and war. ODM presented this as part of an always-unfinished struggle for a very different world. Therein lies its radicalism.

The "culture industry" is perhaps the most famous category of critical theory. It originated in essays by Walter Benjamin and Siegfried Kracauer from the 1930s as well as, most notably, in *Dialectic of Enlightenment* (1944) by Horkheimer and Adorno. But the concept first gained notoriety through ODM. That art was being transformed into a commodity was nothing new, little more than an extension of the logic employed by Marx in the first volume of *Das Kapital* (1867). But the claim that art had lost its uniqueness, its transcendence, its utopian quality, and its ability to foster critical reflection gave the old arguments a new twist. Art now *really* was nothing more than just another commodity. The culture industry would sell anything and turn everything into a fad. Even returning to the classics was impeded by the use of Beethoven or Mozart in advertisements or the transformation of great paintings into posters decorating every other wall in a university dorm. Nor did politics matter. No work of art was immune from the integrative and sanitizing power of the culture industry.

Marcuse sought to infuse a seemingly moribund radicalism degraded by the culture industry with new social priorities and, through Schiller, a new sense of utopian purpose. The former appropriated the "play impulse," "lightness," and the primacy of form from the latter's *Letters on the Aesthetic Education of Man* (1794). Just as Schiller's highlighting of aesthetics served to protect the emancipatory impulse from the bloody politics of the French Revolution, and the ultimate triumph of the Restoration, Marcuse privileged the cultural moment in order to save freedom from authoritarian communism and the technocratic preoccupations of social democracy. The great refusal of the culture industry and what it offered, according to Marcuse, would prevent liberation from becoming identified with "advanced industrial society." He employed this term in the subtitle of ODM and its implication was immediately clear: critical theory intended to target not only capitalist society but "actually existing socialism" and any other production process built upon the "alienation" of labor. That is the justification for introducing the idea of a "new sensibility" and radicalizing E. P. Thompson's claim that the New Left was the first mass movement to place culture at the forefront of the radical enterprise.

Much has been made of the influence (or lack of it) exhibited by ODM. But this much is clear: "Marginal" groups were the catalytic agents for the European strike wave of 1968, and their discourse was decidedly more radical than that of the explicitly liberal civil rights movement in the United States. Much of the New Left was also concerned with what are today termed "post-materialist" issues such as animal rights, personal relations, child rearing, sexuality, and the environment. Infused by what Paul Ricœur termed the "hermeneutic suspicion" of power, these groups also evinced an almost visceral hatred of war, racism, and inequality. The New Left expressed a different aesthetic style that was interconnected with expanding the boundaries of taste, challenging the constrictions of the "culture industry," helping empower previously disenfranchised groups, changing what was permissible, and giving critical education a critical thrust and a lived quality. Conservatives still condemn the 1960s for being the source of "the adversary culture." ODM helped bring that about by challenging radicals to provide what is so sorely missing today: a politics inspired by the ability to imagine a different world and a different aesthetic style of life.

ODM comprehended the conflicts of his epoch in thought, as Hegel might have said, but this is now a different epoch. The closed political universe has reopened. The old consensus is gone. There is hardly a single important moderate or liberal left in the Republican Party and its agenda has basically been set by the Tea Party. Supporters of the free market square off against advocates of state intervention. Ideological cleavages have resurfaced. The happy consciousness is no longer quite so omnipresent. The totally administered society has frayed and new problems present themselves: climate change, economic collapse, neo-fascism, refugees, terror, and the clash of civilizations. The locus of politics has shifted from Europe to the Middle East and China. Once-marginal groups are no longer quite so marginal—and "class" has again become part of the discourse. Experiences of alienation and fears of one-dimensional man, however, still frame our understanding of social reality. It still needs its critics and an unrealized freedom still needs its defenders. Herbert Marcuse's *One-Dimensional Man* remains salient on both counts: it inspires the ongoing redefinition of liberation even as it offers a transformative promise and the utopian dream of a pacified existence.

Part IV

War and Peace

Foreign affairs changed radically since the time Barack Obama first took office. Relatively small numbers of troops still advise organizational clients in Afghanistan, Libya, and among the Syrian opposition, and military aid is still extended to suspect states like Pakistan and Saudi Arabia. In broader terms, questions of national sovereignty and the viability of various Middle Eastern nation-states have taken center stage. President Obama has withstood extraordinary pressure in deciding not to use ground troops in Syria, Ukraine, and elsewhere. Preemptive strikes are no longer justified as they were in the past, international consultation has become a basic element of policy, Israel became subject to much sharper criticism, and negotiation supplanted confrontation in the case of the Iran nuclear treaty. Old shibboleths also fell as President Obama opened relations with Cuba and visited Vietnam and Hiroshima. All of this assumes importance when thinking about responses to new problems that include transnational and transcontinental waves of immigration, religious wars, terrorism on a new scale, and looming environmental threats to the planet. Indeed, this concluding section will, I hope, both provide some insights into American foreign policy as well as a framework for judging future events while linking principles with interests.

22

The Sovereign

It was not long before the Arab Spring turned into a season of discontent. Bereft of the ideological solidarity offered by the mosque and the organizational discipline of the military, incapable of creating strong coalitions and political parties, the democratic revolution produced a crisis of sovereignty. In virtually all nations that were touched by democratic uprisings—Egypt, Iraq, Lebanon, Libya, Mali, Syria, Tunisia, and Yemen—conflict among competing religious/secular, ethnic, or tribal constituencies came to dominate the political landscape. Many in the West considered such turbulence an Oriental or Islamic predilection.[1] In 1848, however, Europe also witnessed spontaneous transnational revolts that, though they also legitimated the principle of parliamentary democracy, were wracked by internal conflicts, as analyzed in Marx's *The Eighteenth Brumaire of Louis Napoleon* (1852), and produced authoritarian governments like those led by Napoleon III and Bismarck. Even worse were the civil wars that emerged as the modern state arose. Ongoing conflicts between France and England during what was known as the Hundred Years War (1337–1453) led to slaughter on a massive scale, while the Thirty Years War (1618–1648) cost Germany and Central Europe about one-quarter of its population in the name of state-building and religious purity.[2] Of course, these primarily religious wars are mostly forgotten (especially by the bigots). Memory is usually jogged only by thoughts of the famous soliloquy from Shakespeare's *Henry V* celebrating the English victory at Agincourt in 1415, Schiller's *Wallenstein* trilogy (1799), or Brecht's "Mother Courage" (1939). Catholics and Protestants butchered one another over the proper road to salvation until finally the resulting Treaty of Osnabruck and the Peace of Westphalia (1648) ushered in the modern nation-state and the controversial concept of sovereignty. The English Civil War (1642–1649) reflected this larger European conflict and, in that context, Thomas Hobbes wrote his *Leviathan* (1651). That book reflected the real-world triumph of the sovereign state.

Sovereignty is predicated on the state's ability to represent the (always elusive) national interest, retain a monopoly over the means of coercion, and supplant the ideological and practical primacy once given to other "private" institutions. The state is sovereign insofar as it can act independently in determining whether it faces a crisis—or not. Sovereignty involves the ability of the state to protect its citizenry that, in the modern context, translates into the delivery of basic public services. To speak of sovereignty then is to speak of political power rendered legitimate by citizens and other regimes—while a *sovereignty deficit* arises from the illegitimacy, or lack of sanctioning power, by the self-styled sovereign. This is not quite as self-evident as it sounds: Sovereignty has an internal and an external character. A state can be recognized as sovereign by its citizens but not by other states (e.g., Palestine) and the alternative is also possible (e.g., Syria or Iraq).

So striking about the contemporary Middle East is the degree to which these two elements of sovereignty are in conflict: it can rarely be established by fiat. In Syria and Iraq but also in Libya, Somalia, and Yemen the state is an imported construct and organic loyalties bound up with sovereignty are missing. Internecine fighting between tribes with private militias is taking place, puppet regimes play at ruling society, and proxy civil wars imperil the citizenry often in the name of combatting ISIS—or its opponent. Following the fall of Colonel Muammar Gaddafi, for example, a unity government of different national factions was proposed for Libya in April 2015 to fight Islamic extremism and create a consensus coalition government. Six months later, however, the nominal national government was asking the Arab League to intervene and state sovereignty had disintegrated. Iran was meanwhile propping up the seemingly established national government of Iraq even while paramilitary organizations were actually ruling different parts of the country. Similar developments had taken place elsewhere and, in fact, Saudi Arabia was often playing both sides against the middle as certain of its sects and tribes were supporting ISIS while the government was trying to win influence over its opponents.

Sovereignty can express itself in many regime types. Whatever the form, however, it must appear as a political phenomenon with final power over public life and its operative laws. All other institutions and associations (whether religious or commercial or ethnic) are private by definition insofar as they express only particular interests. A sovereignty deficit exists when no institution or coalition of organizations representing the particular interests of particular clients can wield power over the citizenry as such and no encompassing institution or organization can fill the power vacuum. Under these circumstances, when power devolves without an institutional point of reference, insecurity at best and civil conflict at worst will necessarily arise. That is, the state must have a monopoly over the means of coercion but also the popular legitimacy to use them in determining and confronting what Carl Schmitt called "the exception" or the emergency situation.

Rarely has a concept been so completely misinterpreted and misused. The exception speaks to any situation where the future of the state hangs in the balance, in short, an emergency. This can be a state of siege, rebellion, or more generally any event that might require reliance on *raison d'état*. Such is the sense in which Schmitt meant that "sovereign is he who decides on the exception." His classic *Political Theology* (1934) was unconcerned with the everyday problems and momentary crises that grip public opinion, and that would make the exception the norm. The point was rather to highlight the sovereign's ability to define a crisis whose defusing or resolution might be likened to the "miracle" of feudal times. It is from the standpoint of the extreme situation that it becomes possible to determine where power lies and how it is exercised in the normal workings of government. Or, to put it another way, the sovereign must have the (coercive) power both to determine when the state is being threatened and the implementation of an appropriate response. That states are susceptible to manipulation by markets (and vice versa) and that private interests can influence public opinion are secondary matters. Understanding the inner dynamics of the concept are what is crucial for making sense of sovereignty and its role in the Middle East.

Hobbes' classic work of political theory privileged both the new state form as sovereign and "the people" as its source of legitimacy. Witnessing the English Civil War and the "long parliament" (1640–1648), which he described in his other great work, *Behemoth* (1681), Hobbes was appalled by the barbaric clash of uncontrolled religious passions and private interests. This he creatively transformed into a "state of nature" marked by the "war of each against all" where the lives of individuals are "poor, nasty, solitary, brutish, and short." Alleviating that condition, he believed, required the existence of a sovereign power. Driven by unrelenting insecurity and fears of death in the state of nature, following the logic of material self-interest, Hobbes assumed those engaged in the untrammeled egoistic violence generated in the state of nature would ultimately prove rational enough to negotiate a "social contract" and choose a sovereign.

Each of them would supposedly prove willing to hand over his rights and powers—and, above all, his arms—to whoever might constrain private passions, enforce stability, and protect lives. The costs must have seemed minimal. Anticipating European liberals in the latter half of the nineteenth century who would support monarchical and authoritarian regimes, so long as they did not interfere with trade, Hobbes believed that the average person was basically unconcerned with politics. Monarchy was unobjectionable since it centralized authority and provided the state with legitimacy. Authoritarianism, in fact, is embedded in Hobbes' political outlook. That would later make him a favorite of staunchly anti-democratic thinkers like Schmitt even though, by highlighting the role of popular sovereignty, Hobbes paved the way for the democratic political theory of John Locke and Jean-Jacques Rousseau.

Schmitt's *The Leviathan in the State Theory of Thomas Hobbes* (1938) is a penetrating study of how Hobbes' great work serves authoritarian purposes as well as illuminates the supposed dangers attendant upon the anti-authoritarian elements of his thinking. Contradicting claims about "the divine right of kings," thereby enraging those same aristocrats and monarchs whose rule he supported, Hobbes justified the sovereign purely in terms of political exigency. He is not necessarily a "great man," he need not have charisma, and he has no particular qualities that either entitle him to his position or that make him different from other citizens. With his emphasis on popular sovereignty, moreover, those excluded from the original social contract (women, people of color, those without property, et al.) can—in principle—demand inclusion. For such reasons, indeed, Hobbes legitimized what would become basic principles of a democratic society.

But his writings harbored authoritarian features that made them appealing to Schmitt and others like him. Hobbes exposed some weaknesses in liberal political theory. How can the asocial criminal types living in the warlike "state of nature" forge a social contract in the first place? Francis Ford Coppola depicted such a scene in *The Godfather III*, where rival gangsters agree to give up their guns before entering a suite to negotiate a common pact—with murderous results. They may have shared a common enemy in the police, but they showed no loyalty to one another, let alone some future sovereign. Hobbes ripped the social contract from history: the state, property, and civil society appear *ex nihilo*. Hobbes also shows how egoism and self-interest (always "rightly understood") provide the foundation of the liberal state and that there is an inherent tension between these attitudes and the public concerns and general interests on which sovereignty relies. These weaknesses in theory became apparent in practice during the Arab Spring.

Holding rebellion in contempt, enmeshed in abstract claims, ignoring prejudice, unconcerned with the exploited, Hobbes' work has had little resonance outside the West. But it teaches many lessons. National liberation coalitions (or "fronts") with disparate beliefs and interests may have fought imperialism, but anti-imperialist solidarity rarely translated into consensual support for a sovereign once the colonizers were defeated. Bloody conflicts between former allies cost hundreds of thousands of lives and shaped much of the post-imperialist world beginning with India/Pakistan and Algeria. Critical of Israel, Hamas and Fatah are today formal partners in a unity coalition while substantively engaged in a civil war. Hobbes' work also provides a warning to imperialists and rebels alike, namely, before overthrowing one sovereign, as was noted previously, another had better be waiting in the wings.

Hobbes understood that the social contract was a purely hypothetical construct designed to provide the sovereign with legitimacy. The old fox was well aware that the sovereign usually came to power through military conquest. But he also recognized that legitimacy was important for any state intent upon transcending particular interests and traditional loyalties. He believed that individuals all share the same fear of death and the same desire for security: all other issues were considered secondary. It led him (mistakenly) to assume that each will place the state above more organic loyalties that he may have for his tribe, ethnic group, class, religion, or family. Commitment to the state is the precondition for citizenship. Hobbes thereby sets the stage for the rigorous distinction between public and private that marks all social contract theorists. The sovereign is the incarnation of "politics" while his subjects contentedly pursue their private business concerns guided by what the Canadian thinker C. B. Macpherson termed "possessive individualism."

Leviathan was the product of a war-weary world. A burgeoning bourgeoisie was advocating the new capitalist mode of production and becoming increasingly contemptuous of old aristocratic prejudices and religious dogmas. This new class understood that the state would incarnate the national will in a way that tribal associations and religious institutions could not. The state became the agent of modernity by generating bureaucracy and the need for expertise, democracy and diversity, science and secularism. But the modernizing process never really took hold outside the Occident, or in the same way, if only because the nation-state was externally imposed upon the

Orient by imperialist powers.[3] That these nations used Arab chieftains to run their colonies obviously didn't help matters. Their interests ran counter to capitalism, nationalism, and state sovereignty.

Modernity blended with traditionalism as multinational oil conglomerates became intertwined with familial monarchies as in Saudi Arabia and the Emirates, while elsewhere the sovereign walked the tightrope between past and present. Nowhere would the state provide a firm sense of identity or generate loyalty for the sovereign. Associated with the British or French imperialist, the putative sovereign was incapable of contesting the traditional feelings of belonging offered by the tribe, ethnicity, or religion. Or, to put it bluntly, the sovereign state was an artificial construct. Its inner workings became corrupt, inefficient, and exploitative, which, in turn, helps explain the appeal of the feudal caliphate demanded by ISIS. This situation continues and the lingering philosophical question is whether the liberal rule of law can be established in forms other than those of the sovereign and secular state.

Fierce battles still rage over what institution should ultimately decide on the exception and the "emergency" situation. Parliaments attempt to make laws that will influence everyday life, but competition between the mosque, the tribe, some paramilitary force, and narrow ethnic organizations interferes. Against claims of sovereignty by the state these institutions attempt to identify their private interests as consonant with the public good. Competition over the exercise of sovereignty expresses nothing more than the sovereignty deficit. Instability is, consequently, built into even the most authoritarian states of the Middle East.

Modernizing military rulers can find themselves in coalition with traditionalists opposing (or supporting) democracy or democratic movements opposing (or supporting) traditionalism. Secular democrats and religious traditionalists can also join together in opposing the military or, as in Egypt following the fall of the hated Mubarak regime, turn against one another and realign against military forces making a bid for sovereignty. Especially in the aftermath of the Arab Spring, traditional ideological alignments often broke down resulting less in compromise than confusion. Institutional preconditions are still lacking for a modern democratic state even while traditionalists remain skeptical about modern politics. Once again, the sovereign is left to reconcile the interests of forces embracing modernity, which are often themselves at odds, with those looking backward to an enchanted past.

For all that, however, Western pundits should not feel smug. Modernizing colonial and military elites often accepted the Western model of the sovereign nation-state in good faith. They wished to break the stranglehold of the sheiks and tribes that ruled the region and condemned it to economic underdevelopment. They saw the breakup of the Ottoman Empire as an opportunity. As colonial protectorates were being constructed, and national boundaries arbitrarily drawn, the ideal of national self-determination seemed to project a new sovereign and a new rallying cry for resisting the exploitative ambitions of the "great powers." National self-determination might contest the hegemony of Islam and legitimate the integration of diverse tribal and religious constituencies such as Christians and the Druze. Modernizing elites also understood that sovereign states were required to nationalize the huge regional oil reserves and maximize the benefits of still unexplored natural resources. Nevertheless, the nation remained an alien construct and an institution incapable of either providing a coherent identity or a coherent division of the region.

The caliphate breaks the connection between the state and the sovereign. Sovereignty becomes a regional matter for what would actually look something like a decentralized confederation held together by religious principles and a version of Sharia law. Its advocates may have skirted institutional issues and questions involving what political agent will decide on the exception or the emergency situation in the last resort. But ISIS has drawn the logical—and radical—conclusion from the existing discontent with modernity and the sovereign state, namely, introduce a pre-modern political formation that will bolster a pre-capitalist understanding of social life and an alternative to the modern (liberal) rule of law in an atavistic theological legal order. Or, to put it another way, ISIS has offered an encompassing political and anti-bureaucratic, socioeconomic, and moral-legal alternative to the Western view of modernity for the Middle East in which the claim to sovereignty has rested on little more than the will to power.

Even that might be saying too much: where imperialist nations once bribed and coerced its local agents, and where multinationals and oil companies built on that foundation, the sovereign today employs similar methods in holding together competing religious, tribal, and ethnic interests. That was clearly the case with Hosni Mubarak in Egypt, Saddam Hussein in Iraq, Hamid Karzai and his successors in Afghanistan, Bashar al-Assad in Syria, and a host of other monarchs and dictators. These supposed sovereigns turned their state bureaucracies into sources of patrimony for the exchange of favors. Economic progress did take place (often as a by-product of the process), consumer goods were introduced, religious institutions felt under siege, and new educational and vocational opportunities opened for women.

But this occurred in concert with omnipresent corruption and, above all, the ever-present threat of political repression.

Little wonder that the authoritarian sovereigns in power prior to the Arab Spring were usually held in contempt or that the traditionalists should have embraced the transnational caliphate with religious foundations. Not simply the liberal or authoritarian state but the sovereign as such became the target not just for urban intellectuals and an incipient bourgeoisie seeking political freedom but also for reactionaries lodged in agrarian constituencies, pre-capitalist classes, and religious institutions, who considered themselves losers (or collateral damage) in the march of progress.

With their traditionalist organic view of society, no less than Carl Schmitt, they viewed sovereignty as irreducible to the mechanical combination of interests that arise in parliamentary democracy. Tensions between urban and secular as against agrarian and religious forces are based not simply on material interests open to compromise by some sovereign power but expressions of religious principle that generate unavoidable violent conflict between "us" and "them." In Iraq and Syria, paramilitary organizations of Sunnis and Shia fighting for power engage in running battles and bombings occur daily. Turf wars between rival tribes (each with its own chieftain) take place in Afghanistan and Libya, while organized gangs enter the mix in Somalia and Yemen. Tightly knit Islamic extremist vanguards like al-Qaeda or Islamic Jihad in the Egyptian Sinai and elsewhere refuse to recognize any more encompassing sovereign power. Yemen has experienced ferocious battles between the Saudi-backed Sunni government and Shia Houthis backed by Iran so that a power vacuum has been created in which al-Qaeda can operate. The implication is clear: the less legitimate the claims of the sovereign, the more absolute the claims of rival religions and tribes, the more probable the success of ideologically motivated paramilitary organizations, and the greater the likelihood of violence.

Western humanitarians as well as hawks require a bit of humility. It has become increasingly clear that foreign intervention cannot redress the sovereignty deficit and produce stability in the Middle East. Citizens of former colonies undoubtedly think less about promises of human rights than Bechtel, XE, or oil companies making a killing. They surely resent the arrogance of those who (once again) deny them the possibility of developing their own traditions while forgetting that it took more than a century-long bloodbath to secure the triumph of the sovereign state in Europe. Once-colonized peoples will not be happy about foreign soldiers dictating events, entering their homes, desecrating their mosques, ruining their economy, and killing their friends. Intervention tends to weaken sovereignty almost by definition.

Unrealistic realists often refer admiringly to the tough-minded Hobbes. They draw from him the implication that, since there is no sovereign, a war-like state of nature exists in the international arena. That makes foreign intervention necessary and ethical constraints on political action superfluous. Europe can remain content with following Kantian ethics while championing diplomacy and international law, given its reduced power and status, but the United States must embrace the Hobbesian outlook and power politics.[4] Ironically, however, these realists ignore Hobbes' most basic lesson, namely, that only chaos and bloodshed can come from dislodging a sovereign without having a legitimate substitute waiting in the wings. That has certainly been the story of American involvement in Afghanistan and Iraq. It was also the case in Libya where the attack at Benghazi, along with half a dozen others that received less media coverage, served as responses to an American-assisted rebellion in which thousands were killed and a power vacuum accompanied by the usual sovereignty deficit resulted. Echoing the quip by Eric Hobsbawm, the great historian, indeed, "nothing is more dangerous than a superpower that claims it is doing the world a favor."

Intervention has become what David Bromwich has called a "rationalized addiction" for the United States. Justifications for intruding upon the sovereignty of other states or imposing a sovereign are usually based on preventing chaos, protecting human rights, or serving the national interest. But they are hollow. Statistics conflict—though they are all frightening. As of March 2015, American intervention in Afghanistan and Iraq together has resulted in 210,000 civilians killed, nearly 1.5 million wounded, roughly double that number in exiles, wrecked economies, unimaginable environmental devastation, and ongoing civil strife in the Middle East as a whole; since 9/11, 4 million people have died.[5] That all of this somehow furthers human rights (even in the long run) is a disingenuous claim to make—especially when others pay the price. The American supported overthrow of Gaddafi facilitated the flow of arms and troops across Libya's border as well as a new wave of African immigration. It is also difficult to argue that the American national interest has been served when roughly 6,900 American soldiers have been killed, 900,000 wounded, and $4 trillion have been spent for seemingly no purpose.[6] Use of torture, mercenaries, and rendition have also undermined the moral standing of the United States and, by subverting the sovereignty of other nations, generated feelings of national humiliation that will take a long time to disappear.

The leviathan looms large. The difficulties of transferring an Occidental construct into an Oriental context have become ever more apparent. But few thinkers are as relevant as Hobbes for analyzing sovereignty and its preconditions. To condemn him for the current state of nature or the new authoritarian tendencies in the Middle East is to kill the messenger. If nothing else, the Arab Spring suggests that there is a deep desire on the part of many in the region to shape their future in democratic fashion. Some obstacles standing in the way of sovereignty derive from the decisions of foreign powers but others are domestic in origin. Long after colonialism has faded, the Arab world is still being denied the chance to develop on its own, make its own mistakes, and generate its own institutions appropriate to the modern age. Securing popular sovereignty in the people is always difficult where church blends with state and so much of the political structure appears little more than an artificial construct. But such is the hand that has been dealt. It is from that context alone that the new sovereign will arise, hopefully, responsible to those alone who should count: the citizenry.

23

The Forest and the Trees

The United States in Afghanistan

Appearance is everything: General David Petraeus, who once commanded American forces in Afghanistan, stated that he would not preside over a "graceful exit" from that beleaguered country and that he might oppose withdrawal (*New York Times*, 16 August 2010). His words echoed the sentiments expressed time and again by Lyndon B. Johnson and Richard Nixon about Vietnam. These presidents, too, did not wish to lose a war that could not be won.[1] Vanity and misguided political calculation again confront the national interest. While Iraq is written off, though bombings and attacks are still frequent, the same assumptions that guided the earlier debacle are retained in American policy toward Afghanistan. Shards of criticism about this or that mistake or defeat or miscalculation make the news. Day after day there are reports concerning victories and retreats, an enemy offensive stalled and territory lost, general improvements and decline in security, unabated corruption and successful elections—and the ongoing danger of new American slippage into an old quagmire. But there is no overview. It is really a matter of the forest not the trees.

The stage was set for the present conflict in 1979 when the United States supported the mujahideen (and the young Osama bin Laden) in their struggle against the Soviet Union. That phase of the conflict ended when the Soviet Union collapsed and, from 1989 until 2001, the United States found itself jockeying for influence by entering into temporary and complex coalitions with certain warlords fighting for control of the country. Ultimately, however, the Taliban seized power. And so matters stood until 9/11/2001. President George W. Bush initially entered into negotiations with the ruling Taliban in order to secure the capture of Osama bin Laden, who had masterminded the attack against the World Trade Center.

Rumors persist to this day that the criminal had been cornered and that he escaped only because of bureaucratic infighting over which military or political leader would claim credit for the catch. In any event, however, the invasion of Iraq led the United States to shift its priorities. Warlords went back to fighting for power in Afghanistan, Osama went into hiding, and the Taliban regrouped. The failure of the Iraqi invasion left the United States without a secure foothold in the region, and in 2009, copying the "surge" policy employed in Iraq, President Barack Obama decided to send thirty thousand new troops into Afghanistan over the next six months in anticipation of a withdrawal eighteen months later. Supporters use the surge as an argument for "more" troops (everywhere), though no domestic agent or ally is specified, other than the illegitimate sovereign of the moment. The willingness of President Obama to widen the rules of engagement in 2016 has dangerous implications for the United States since it is becoming ever more apparent that a "military solution" is impossible.

Afghanistan borders Pakistan and provides a pathway into Iran and the host of nations known as "the -stans." Oil interests—as usual—come into play: an oil pipeline capable of connecting different parts of the region would run through Afghanistan. But that oft-discussed prospect lies far down the road. Considerations about the geopolitical importance of Afghanistan and the thought of the Taliban in power led yet again to a policy of neither war nor peace and "minimal" engagement. Afghanistan is not the only country, however, in which the United States is currently engaged. Fifty thousand soldiers remain stationed in Iraq and American drones are striking Pakistan and elsewhere in the region. That doesn't change the stark reality: Afghanistan and Iraq will have cost the United States $4 trillion—not to speak of lives lost—well over four times the amount the United States spent on fighting the Soviet Union at the end of the Cold War.[2] The United States still has bases in Afghanistan, Pakistan, Kazakhstan, Uzbekistan, Tajikistan, and Kyrgyzstan. Goods and materials in Afghanistan are still mostly outsourced through private companies like XE (formerly known as Blackwater) with military commodities supplied by Kestrel Technologies. "Cadillac mercenaries," as the soldiers of these private corporations have been called, still treat Afghani and Iraqi citizens with disdain, and their lack of accountability remains a prime source of tension between the United States and its supposed benefactors.

Capturing Osama bin Laden was a symbolic victory but it didn't help stabilize Afghanistan, marginalize the Taliban, or quell the spread of terrorism. Why should the Afghani people consider the United States as anything other than a new imperialist invader? From Alexander the Great to the British to the Russians and now to the United States—Afghanistan has been under attack and threat of invasion.[3] Supporters of American policy insist that the United States is less an invader than a partner and that, through the surge in its troop levels combined with its effective use of drone missiles, the Taliban is now weaker than before. The United States has also stated its willingness to work with virtually any leadership (excluding the Taliban) and that its "counter-insurgency" program is less preoccupied with military victory than reconstructing Afghani society.[4] Between 2002 and 2015 the United States spent around $110 billion to rebuild Afghanistan.[5] And it remains the case that more than half the children in the country are malnourished.[6] Today as in 2010: "Pick a measurement affecting ordinary Afghans and the record since November 2001 when Kabul fell to Allied forces is likely to show stagnation or setbacks and, almost invariably, suffering."[7]

Constructing a new civil society in Afghanistan remains predicated on renovating the army and the police forces. But the lack of success is notable: security has deteriorated in much of the country as of 2016 thereby hampering both overall stability and humanitarian aid.[8] Taliban infiltration is a constant worry and incompetence is an even bigger one, drug addiction is rampant, and Afghanistan has one of the lowest literacy rates in the world.[9] All this makes increasing troop levels tempting in the military and police and instituting anti-corruption courts. The Afghani military is seen as ultimately comprising a force of about 200,000 and the police as comprising about 157,000 as of 2015. Add the 100,000 private contractors, 50,000 American troops, and 45,000 NATO troops that existed in 2010, and a vision of Afghanistan takes shape.[10]

Numbers don't lie. The need for such an abundance of troops testifies to the strength of the Taliban, and it appears that the United States is still less engaged in reconstructing civil society than creating an armed camp. Afghanistan lacks a bureaucratic infrastructure and 90 percent of its state spending is funded by foreign assistance. In 2016, roughly twenty-one out of twenty-seven million Afghanis are either "food-insecure" or "borderline food-insecure,"[11] and unemployment increased from 25 percent to 40 percent from 2014 to 2015.[12] Corruption is beyond rampant: elections are plagued by fraud and payoffs to voters, the currency is almost worthless, and it is an open secret that the families of presidents and vice presidents are taking massive bribes. Economic growth increased from 1.3 percent in 2014 to 1.5 percent in 2015 and private consumption has dipped.[13]

These are dismal conditions in which a "republic" is to take root—if that is even the intent any longer. American foreign policy is still caught between seeking to defeat the Taliban by military means, seeking to introduce civil society, and nation-building. Even while creating an armed camp the United States is attempting to stabilize entire regions of Afghanistan rather than just towns and villages. A successful counter-insurgency strategy, however, requires a reliable political partner committed to building a democratic state. But that does not exist either. Ambassador Karl W. Eikenberry has stated that the former president Karzai was "not an adequate strategic partner" and that his legitimacy was incapable of strengthening the sovereignty of Afghanistan (*New York Times*, 26 January 2010). The situation has not changed because the role of the sovereign has not changed: he remains a bagman or—more generously—mediator between the United States and the more important warlords in Afghanistan. The drug trade now accounts for about 50 percent of the GNP,[14] and in 2010 it was estimated that bribery equals roughly one-quarter of the GDP—and that it would keep growing.[15]

But it gets worse. American policy is still working with the assumption that a traditional agrarian society with non-Western roots can simply be "modernized" in accordance with some western model. Afghanistan rests on insular tribal and kinship systems and everyday politics is local in the most extreme sense. Thirty languages and dozens of dialects are spoken in Afghanistan and the country is composed of seven major ethnic groups. The Tajiks, Uzbeks, and Pashtuns are the most prominent with the latter controlling roughly 40 percent of the country and serving as the base for the Taliban. There is no functioning bureaucracy, the existing state lacks a monopoly over the means of coercion, and national solidarity exists as a form of negative integration—or, more simply, as a source of opposition to the imperialist enemy. Given the lack of a recognized sovereign, in fact, the Taliban often assumes the guise of something like a national liberation front—and it obviously benefits from the undeniable fact that religion is the only ideology capable of generating positive integration in a traditional society.

There is also a way in which current thinking is predicated on a new version of the "domino theory" that so many embraced during the Vietnam War. With little exaggeration, it was suggested that, should Saigon fall to the Communists, the rest of Southeast Asia would follow, next would come Australia, and—soon enough—California would be subject to attack. A slightly more sober variant of this clearly paranoid kind of thinking is now in play: Should the Taliban gain control of Afghanistan, the next country to fall would be Pakistan. Further intervention is being justified by various reports from the National Intelligence Council, and the CIA suggested that, by 2015, Pakistan might yet become another failed state—and it seems that has become the case. With its seventy to ninety nuclear missiles, courtesy of the Bush administration, this would have serious implications for the region and the world. The existence of Taliban bases in Pakistan can be legitimately seen as constituting a threat to any sovereign government in Afghanistan. In seeking to prevent a victory of the Taliban in Afghanistan, however, American policy might itself be contributing to the destabilization of Pakistan. A five-year package approaching $7.5 billion in overwhelmingly military aid was provided in 2009 for Pakistan, which cast a large shadow over its weak civil society, even while the United States was strengthening its alliance with India.

Pakistan has traditionally seen Afghanistan as an element of its India policy. Even ten years ago, it was reasonable to assume that Pakistan would count on the Taliban as a potential ally against India. Meanwhile the almost daily drone attacks on Taliban and al-Qaeda bases in ever-expanding areas of Pakistan, along with North and South Waziristan, are interpreted by everyday Pakistanis as an attack on their country's sovereignty. Enough experts have asserted that the rise of Pashtun nationalism, the new prominence of the Taliban, and even the increase in suicide bombings, is a direct function of the growing American presence in the country.[16] Splits between Sunni and Shiite Muslims have also produced ongoing tensions between Afghanistan and Iran. The situation is fluid, incalculable, and complex. The question naturally arises: Is the current policy toward Afghanistan in the American national interest?

With his speech at West Point in December of 2009, President Obama stated that the United States was now involved in "a war of necessity." By the same token, however, he showed wariness about yet another open-ended war and he stated that American troops would be home before the 2010 elections. But this was actually an evasion. And, in 2016, a new expansion of the American presence seemed possible. The former exit strategy encouraged the Taliban to hang on until the United States left. It also encouraged Pakistan to maintain subterranean relations with militants opposed to India in Afghanistan, Baluchistan, and Kashmir. The United States wound up in a no-win situation: it will appear imperialistic if it stays and weak if it leaves. Staying will obviously involve increased troop levels and regionally enmesh the United States all over again. But there is no reason to believe either that American influence will grow or that Americans will support this kind of policy. Justifications are vague at best and the political risks are palpable: staying would ultimately involve embracing failed policies while expecting a different outcome.

American policy in Afghanistan shows the importance of having clear goals in the pursuit of the national interest. The United States is showing its weakness, conceptually as well as militarily. There is no conviction animating this struggle. American allies in Afghanistan have been bought. Embracing the lesser evil against the Taliban is a foolish strategy when the chances for success are meager, the costs are great, genuine support for a foreign military force is lacking, and corrupt tribal loyalties are in play. American geopolitical interests have never been clarified. Even the deputy director of the CIA, Paul R. Pillar, was unconvinced that the withdrawal of foreign troops will significantly increase the threat of terrorist attacks by the Taliban upon Western nations.[17] Either geopolitical interests can be stated clearly and simply, without artifice, or they are probably not real interests at all. The degree to which such interests can be stated simply and clearly, without pretense or lying, is the degree to which a citizenry might support them. The only real American interest in the course currently being pursued in Afghanistan is that of the military and the parasitical companies and advisors that leech off it. They know it and, increasingly, the American public knows it as well. The growing public disillusionment concerns not only the conduct of the war but its lack of material and moral purpose. In the aftermath of Iraq, and perhaps since Vietnam, the American government can no longer presuppose a quiescent citizenry that will rubber-stamp its foreign adventures. Critique has a new role to play. Speaking truth to power now rests not merely upon cultivating political knowledge but also on a clear sense of political purpose.

24

Talking in Tehran

Jointly sponsored by US Academics for Peace and the Institute for Political and International Studies in Tehran, ten American university professors and theologians were invited to visit Iran from January 19 to 26, 2014. Negotiations had just been concluded between Iran and the bloc of six world powers (PS 5+1), including the United States, on the basic framework for an interim treaty with respect to the Iranian nuclear program. That treaty paved the way for the final product that was formalized in June of 2015. From the first, it sparked a storm of controversy. While awaiting confirmation by the Senate, tempers flared. That was especially the case in the United States where, spurred by Israeli prime minister Benjamin Netanyahu's public intervention in the confirmation debate, Zionist organizations sponsored full-page ads in venues like the New York Times calling upon all senators to join Senator Charles Schumer (D-NY) and "kill the deal with Iran before Iranian nukes kill millions of Americans."

Kourosh Ziabari conducted this interview with me for the *Tehran Times* on April 9, 2014, to assess the interim nuclear accord between and the prospects of Iran-West relations following the election of President Hassan Rouhani to succeed Mahmoud Ahmadinejad, whose notoriety had much to do with his explicit anti-American and anti-Semitic pronouncements. What follows is the text of that interview.

Q: You were part of a delegation of American academics that traveled to Iran to confer with the Iranian university professors, students, and officials with the aim of mending the marred and blemished relations between Iran and the United States. Please tell us more about the objectives of this trip and your plans and programs in Iran.

A: I visited Iran with a delegation organized by US Academics for Peace. Under the stewardship of Dr. James Jennings, its members previously visited Iraq before the American invasion, Iran, Syria, and Sudan/Darfur. The purpose was always to improve cultural relations between the United States and some country from which it was estranged. In Iran, we met with a deputy foreign minister, officials from various ministries, and held seminars with representatives of the Institute for Political and International Studies. Worth noting is that our visit had the backing of Foreign Minister Mohammad Javad Zarif and we had the privilege of spending a few hours in meetings with one of the chief Iranian negotiators on nuclear issues. Our trips all attempted to improve communication, better understanding, offer a different political perspective back home through our media contacts, and also lay the basis for further cultural exchanges and common research projects.

Q: What's your evaluation of the public sphere of Iran, the state of daily life in the streets of Tehran, the Iranian lifestyle and the people's interaction with each other? How has Iran changed since the last time you visited the country?

A: My sense was that the new administration of President Rouhani has provided, at least those people I met, with new hope for improving ties with the West and the United States, thereby lessening sanctions and improving economic life, but also with respect to expanding cultural freedom. There is clearly more political polarization and (perhaps it follows) there are actually more political prisoners than under the old regime. More have certainly been executed than under Ahmadinejad. Of course, when it comes to prisoners, the United States should not be pointing fingers—its prison-industrial complex has incarcerated more people (and overwhelmingly people of color) than any state other than South Africa. In any event, if Iran opens to the West, then the state will probably become less stringent. Beyond this, however, we experienced a new optimism and glimpsed a new window of opportunity for bettering relations between our countries.

Q: Why is it important for the academicians, journalists, and other professionals both in Iran and the United States to interact and have cultural exchanges with each other? Do you believe that these exchanges can eliminate misunderstandings and pave the way for the improvement of Iran-U.S. relations in the diplomatic level?

A: Civic diplomacy or what has been termed "soft diplomacy" usually has only indirect effects. But that does not invalidate its importance. Better understanding is more than a cliché: our visits to different Islamic nations taught us how little we know about Arab public opinion and political attitudes toward the United States and, by the same token, how little is known in the Middle East about American politics and the conflicting attitudes of our citizenry. Ignorance often has an impact upon policy. Especially right-wing American policymakers miscalculated the cultural climate in expecting to be welcomed with open arms in Iraq and similar miscalculations occurred in Afghanistan and Syria. As far as Iran is concerned, we were somewhat surprised by the lack of knowledge about the complexities of American politics, such as the splits within the Democratic Party and even within the Jewish community, not only among everyday citizens but experts as well.

Q: How do you assess the recent interim nuclear accord between Iran and the six world powers, including the United States? For the first time in more than three decades, the presidents of Iran and the United States talked on the phone while their foreign ministers conferred a number of times. What's your assessment of the agreement that was struck in Geneva and the upcoming talks in Vienna for reaching a comprehensive solution?

A: Ideological posturing and crude stereotyping marked the nuclear controversy from its inception. According to international law, Iran has the right to develop nuclear energy for domestic uses. In America, however, this right has been ignored and my country's policy has been deeply influenced by fears of Iranian ambitions and fanaticism that rest on stereotypical assumptions. Even with a nuclear bomb, and the ability to deliver it, Israel is estimated to have four hundred such weapons and the United States has thousands. Our hosts at IPIS stated categorically that Iran knows it will be committing suicide should it attack either Israel or the United States. They also noted that there is no regional target for an Iranian attack: Syria, Iraq, Afghanistan, and even Pakistan are all fracturing and in disarray. Iran is already the major power in the region (outside of Israel and perhaps Saudi Arabia). Iran has also never had imperialist ambitions in the modern era. It may lend support to Shiites fighting in Lebanon, Syria, and Yemen, but that is about it. It is doing no more, and probably much less, than either Saudi Arabia or the United Arab Emirates. I would like to find out what Israeli prime minister Netanyahu means when he speaks about Iran posing an "existential threat"—other than that he simply *feels* afraid. That sentiment is not exactly sufficient to justify bombing Iran: it might be more useful to consider that the annihilation of Iran would leave Israel unchallenged in its regional dominance.

But that, of course, is not the way things are being portrayed. What the recent accord represents, in my opinion, is the first step in bracketing stereotypes and prejudices. The agreement challenges the old view of Iran as a terrorist state entangled in the axis of evil. I am no scientist and I cannot speak to the details of the nuclear accord, but I can say that, while a comprehensive resolution of tensions between our countries will prove difficult, the new rapprochement is a beginning. We should recognize it for what it is: the first encounter between Iran and the United States in thirty-five years and a possible first step in reorienting Occidental-Oriental relations.

Q: The delegation that traveled to Tehran last month consisted of a number of academics from different fields, including theology, and religion. Do you think that the elimination of mistrust and hostilities between Iran and the United States might also pave the way for a more comprehensive interfaith dialogue between the Muslims and Christians? Is the improvement of Iran-U.S. bilateral ties going to contribute to the abolition of Islamophobic sentiments by presenting a fairer and more balanced image of Islam to the American society?

A: I am tempted to put it the other way around. Given the role of religion in the Middle East, reconciliation between differing faiths is perhaps *the* precondition for eliminating all other forms of mistrust. We hope that a new interfaith dialogue will take place and US Academics would be delighted to participate. It seems to me that furthering religious tolerance is part of any genuine lessening of tensions and attempting to deal with other political conflicts not merely between Christians and Muslims but also between Sunni and Shia. Destructive stereotypes that equate Islam with a "gutter religion" play a particularly important role and combating them is another reason for greater cultural awareness and interchange. There must also be a reason why Iran has supported the Houthis in Yemen, Assad in Syria, and Hezbollah in Lebanon. Progressive politics in the region cannot ignore the religious variable. That is also true from the standpoint of Iran. The United States was never the "great Satan" and Islamophobia does not rule the United States. It has actually receded somewhat, especially in the cities. Nevertheless, this prejudice like any other remains in reserve—ready for political manipulation.

Q: What was the reaction and perception of the American academics that visited Iran for the first time? What did they think of Iran? What did they say on returning to the States? Had their preconceptions changed after coming to Iran?

A: Most of my colleagues who visited Iran for the first time were delighted by the kind treatment that they experienced in Tehran. Their counterparts were sophisticated, reasonable, and curious about the United States. Our delegation saw a bustling city with its bazaar, museums, and restaurants. But we also saw that sanctions had an economic impact. Our hosts noted that the present moment offered a "window of opportunity" that could close quickly—and our delegation took these warnings very seriously. Upon returning to the United States, we gave interviews, wrote letters to newspapers, held public lectures, opened journals to Iranian academics, and began to talk about future delegations and conferences. All of us did what was in our power to better relations between our countries.

Q: Does the improvement of bilateral ties between Iran and the United States in all fields lead to greater security and peace in the Middle East? Will the other nations in this turbulent region benefit from a thaw in Iran-U.S. relations?

A: The change that has taken place in Iranian foreign policy is mirrored by the change in my own country. I understand that American drones have cost far too many lives, that Guantanamo is still open (congressional votes are necessary to close it), and that American policy remains entangled with the interests of various reactionary regimes. But it is also the case that President Obama has rejected the "preemptive strike" doctrine of the Bush administration, that he has withdrawn the great bulk of forces from Afghanistan and Iraq, that he has followed a prudent course in Syria, that the number of nuclear warheads in the world has actually gone down, that he has been sharply critical of Israel, and that he has withstood immense pressure by AIPAC and politicians from both parties calling upon him to bomb Iran. The American citizenry is sick of war and sick of interventions without plan or purpose. The president knows that security does not simply emanate from the barrel of a gun and that meaningful peace not only in Syria but in the region as a whole is impossible without Iran. Furthering peace requires a cosmopolitan dialogue—and I hope that US Academics can contribute to it.

Kourosh Ziabari is an award-winning Iranian journalist and reporter. He has won three awards in Iran's National Press Festival. He is the recipient of the Senior Journalists Seminar 2015 Fellowship by the Hawaii-based East-West Center. He has also been granted the Gabriel Garcia Marquez Fellowship in Cultural Journalism by the FNPI foundation in Colombia in November 2015. Kourosh is the Iran-based correspondent and reporter of Fair Observer, *an international media corporation in California comprising more than 1,500 contributors worldwide. A staff writer of* Iran Review *news and analysis website, he contributes to* The Huffington Post, Middle East Eye, Your Middle East, *and* International Policy Digest *and is an AMENDS Global Fellow at Stanford University.*

25

America's Israel

American foreign policy has undergone a qualitative change since Barack Obama took over the presidency from George W. Bush. It's not all rosy. Hundreds of drone strikes costing thousands of lives have taken place in Libya and Pakistan. Guantanamo is still open. Skeletal forces remain in Afghanistan and Iraq—and (as of 2011) more than one thousand American bases dot the planet. Without discounting the waste of resources and lives, however, there is a bigger picture. Preemptive strikes are no longer the first option, the defense budget has been cut, military action in Syria has been avoided, Iran has not been bombed and (for the first time in thirty-five years) negotiations with its government are underway: a nuclear deal has been signed and there is an opening for common action on many fronts in the Middle East. There is less talk about an axis of evil and a war on terror—almost all of this to the chagrin of the Israeli government led by Prime Minister Benjamin Netanyahu whose public attempts to subvert nuclear negotiations with Iran and intervene in the formation of American foreign policy were a disaster. Israel's policy of expanding settlements and its stalling of the peace process were openly criticized by President Obama, who is detested by Israeli hardliners in spite of what will probably turn into a $38 billion aid package over ten years. A "framework" for peace is now on the table that focuses on the West Bank in endorsing a two-state solution to the Israeli-Palestinian conflict.

Many will claim that this is all too little and too late. UN condemnations of Israel are still vetoed by the United States, $60 million in support for UNESCO was withdrawn in 2011 when Palestine was admitted to the organization, and the Obama administration remains unwilling to officially recognize Palestine as a state in its current form. Hamas is still considered a terrorist organization, its effective exclusion from the current peace process bodes ill, and—above all—American military support for

Israel in the event of an armed conflict is a forgone conclusion. That is unlikely to change. According to the *Defense News* (Gannett), published in August 2013, Congress has provided Israel with $3.175 billion in military aid in grants and loans per year until 2017. The money is considered well spent—and the amount might well go up. With roots in Cold War thinking, when Israel appeared as a bulwark against the seemingly radical Arab States and (supposedly communist) movements of national liberation in the Middle East, the belief still exists among most mainstream politicians in the United States, conservative and liberal, that unquestioning support for Israel is fundamental to the national interest.

Why? Complex feelings mix compassion and guilt when it comes to Israel and the Holocaust. There is identification as well as empathy for the Jew since the usual bourgeois or middle-class portrayal tends to make him or her appear "just like us"—Anne Frank is a case in point—as against the Palestinian who is very unlike us. Few Americans have any idea about the trauma (*nakba*) experienced by the more than 650–700,000 Arabs expelled from their land by Israelis during the war of 1947–1948. Zionist myths still persist about Israel as having been "a land without a people for a people without a land." Some also still believe in stereotypes emanating from films like *Exodus*, romanticize the shtetl, and identify with characters like Tevye the Milkman. An interesting expression of the most basic friend/enemy distinction thus comes into play. After 9/11, indeed, not only Jews fear the impending pogrom supposedly being plotted by Arab barbarians at the gate.

But Israel has now existed as a colonial power for twice as long as the tiny state that arose in 1948. It is a leading military power with a sophisticated army and an estimated stockpile of three to four hundred nuclear weapons. The Israeli economy is not labor intensive and it is robust. Yet Israel is by far the greatest recipient of American foreign (military) aid, double the amount given Egypt, the second greatest recipient. Many justify this privileging by insisting that Israel is the only democratic state in the Middle East—or, somewhat less liberally, the only non-Arabic and non-Islamic state in the region. But Israeli democracy bears marked similarities to that of South Africa under apartheid—or perhaps the American South prior to the civil rights movement. World public opinion now considers Israel's treatment of the Palestinians as grossly inhumane and even criminal. That is particularly the case with the "open air prison" of Gaza where ironically, at the behest of the West, democratic elections were held in 2006. The result was a resounding victory for Hamas that was totally unforeseen by Western experts.

Support for Israel by the United States has seemed unflinching. But it was only in 1967 that Israel and America established their bond. Only with Israel's military victory in 1967 would Israel appear as a genuinely attractive ally. Israel's military strength (not its weakness) attracted the United States. Its geopolitical value proved decisive. That value has declined along with the influence of the United States in the wake of its invasions of Afghanistan and Iraq. Its original view of the region was provincial and shortsighted. It seems almost obvious that better relations are necessary with Arab and Islamic states in the region. Nevertheless, former speaker of the house Tip O'Neill liked to say that in America "all politics is local politics."

More is involved here than the oft-noted indifference to foreign affairs by the voting public (except, of course, when the United States is directly affected). The American political system is one in which political parties are weak and organized interests are strong. It is federal in nature and it is built on single-member districts in which the winner takes all. This means that each candidate is left to his own devices. Money by itself is not the issue. Politically motivated Jews are organized, they mostly support Israeli policies, and they have a host of lobbying organizations. They vote, and their vote is particularly important in cities in large states with many electoral votes in presidential campaigns such as California, Florida, Illinois, New Jersey, and New York. Most of these states have any number of powerful liberal representatives, like Senator Charles Schumer (D-NY) or Senator Diane Feinstein (D-CA) or Senator Robert Menendez (D-NJ). But it would be more precise to say that they are liberal on most issues other than those that concern Israel. And that only makes sense. Arabs do not vote, and they lack strong lobbying organizations. There is no conspiracy at work: it is simply that, even were Jewish lobbies not to give a cent in donations, obvious political incentives exist for American politicians to support Israeli rather than Palestinian interests.

Local concerns trump the national interest in Congress and, if only for this reason, President Obama has been careful in pursuing his agenda in the Middle East. His office lifts his outlook beyond the local, but that is true only to a certain point. Other domestic and foreign policy issues exist for which he needs congressional support, and the Israeli-Palestinian conflict makes log-rolling and deal-making on these other issues more difficult. President Obama can count on neither mainstream Democrats nor Republicans in developing a more radical policy for the Middle East (or for pressuring Israel through cuts in foreign aid) and he certainly cannot count on the Islamophobic far right that includes many Christian fundamentalists and members of the Tea Party. With public pressure, perhaps something more progressive can come out of Washington. Some thoughtful liberal politicians might then change their views. Sympathy for Palestine has slowly been growing among the American public due to the publicity and work of organizations like US Campaign Against the Occupation, Code Pink, and supporters of Boycott Divestment Sanctions (BDS). But the critics remain in the minority. That is why expanding public debate about the Israeli-Palestinian conflict is so important, why demonstrations are necessary, why attacking the bigoted stereotypes and prevalent political myths is crucial, why disseminating information is not just an academic enterprise, and why—above all—it needs to be made clear that the American national interest will be served only when Israel is judged on its actions and treated as one state among others.

26

Closing the Deal

America, Iran, and the Nuclear Treaty of 2015

For the first time since the overthrow of the Shah and the establishment of the Iranian Republic more than thirty-five years ago, the United States and Iran have talked with one another in civil tones rather than bellicose rhetoric. The result was the treaty of 2015 concerning the future of nuclear energy (and perhaps the prospect of a nuclear weapon) in Iran that was born of compromise and attempts to allay suspicions on the domestic front in both countries. Historical context for the signing is crucial. Intense mutual distrust began following the prominent role played by the United States in overthrowing the democratic regime of Mohammad Mosaddegh in 1953 (primarily for nationalizing its oil companies) and installing the Shah Mohammad Reza Pahlavi, hated by the populace as both an American puppet and a decadent despot. U.S.-Iranian relations consequently plummeted when in 1979 he was overthrown by the first successful Islamic revolution that was led by Ayatollah Khomeini.

The Shah and his family sought refuge in the United States as, more for symbolic than practical reasons, the American Embassy was occupied amid chants of "Death to America" and others demanding the annihilation of Israel. Hostages were taken, attempts to free them failed, and the United States stood humiliated before the rest of the world as Ronald Reagan replaced Jimmy Carter as president. While the new theocratic republic took shape, relations between the United States and Iran deteriorated further. American support for the invasion of Iran by Saddam Hussein's Iraq only strengthened earlier feelings of national hatred and mistrust. This misguided attempt at geopolitics identified the United States with a brutal aggressor in a war that lasted from 1980 to 1988 and cost the lives of nearly a million soldiers and civilians. Worse: the borders basically remained unchanged, thereby generating frustration and incessant rumors of a Western conspiracy directed against one country or the other along with a revanchist spirit in both. With its support of Iraq, where Saddam's Sunni government was repressing the nation's Shia majority, and its hostility to both Syria and Iran, as well as its close ties to Saudi Arabia, it appeared that the United States had made the geopolitical decision to side with Sunnis against Shia in a simmering conflict with regional implications.

As if to confirm the point, the United States and its European allies soon introduced sanctions that economically isolated Iran from the West, strangled what there was of its indigenous bourgeoisie, and ultimately led the republic to embrace a nuclear strategy. It also heightened the domestic power of the mosque and the Revolutionary Guards. Anti-American and anti-Israeli demonstrations took place throughout the country. Economic miseries in Iran were meanwhile blamed on the United States and Israel, which then labeled Iran a "rogue" state and a participant in President George W. Bush's "axis of evil." Holocaust denial and extremist rhetoric only seemed to validate this impression.

Ironically, the situation only grew worse with the American invasions of Afghanistan and Iraq. Little sympathy was spent by Iran on the plight of its former enemy. Yet simply bombing Iraq, thereby leaving Iran as the dominant Islamic power in the region, made little strategic sense. It seemed only logical that these invasions were merely the first steps of a larger plan to assert American/Israeli hegemony in the Middle East; indeed, this standpoint only gained new support in Iran and elsewhere following the implosion of Syria. Iran seemed the only nation left capable of opposing the United States (and Israel)—and it felt surrounded. American troops were stationed in Afghanistan and Iraq; American nuclear technology had been sent to India and Pakistan. American military packages were given not only to Israel but also to Saudi Arabia, Egypt, and Jordan. Iran was thus left economically isolated and militarily encircled, demeaned for its imperialist ambitions and wild anti-Semitism, and denied the right to develop its own nuclear program by the only nation to ever employ atomic weapons in wiping out Hiroshima and Nagasaki to end World War II.

Given this history, the lack of support from a single Senate Republican, and the disaffection of many Democrats, it was amazing that President Barack Obama was able to move forward on this treaty between Iran and the five nations in the UN Security Council plus Germany (P5+1). An earlier attempt had taken place in Paris in 2004. But the United States did not participate, while the bellicose rhetoric opposing the treaty by Mahmoud Ahmadinejad turned him into a celebrity at home and strengthened the anti-Western right wing of Iranian politics. Negotiations thus came to nothing, and Iran effectively became an outcast. That changed with the initiatives taken by President Obama and the new regime led by President Hassan Rouhani and his foreign minister, Javad Zarif. The contours of the deal forged by Kerry and Zarif are overloaded with detail but relatively easy to grasp: Iran cuts its stockpile of medium-enriched uranium and virtually eliminates its low-enriched uranium, refuses to build heavy water facilities, and drastically reduces its centrifuges for fifteen years. Uranium enrichment is limited to domestic uses, and the International Atomic Energy Agency is given access to agreed-upon sites. In exchange, the United States and Europe immediately lift their sanctions, thereby allowing an estimated $150 billion in investments and trade to flow into Iran.

Once again, Iran would not be allowed to produce weapons-grade fuel for fifteen years; it would permit on-site inspections by international agencies; and, in exchange, the P5+1 would allow low nuclear enrichment for domestic purposes and lift all sanctions with all due speed. Critics among Democrats from large urban areas like Senator Chuck Schumer (D-NY), who vote liberal on virtually every issue except Israel, right-wing evangelicals, and a Republican Party dominated by the Tea Party, as well as Israeli prime minister Benjamin Netanyahu and a phalanx of Zionist interest groups led by AIPAC, began a sensational and well-funded campaign to subvert the treaty in Congress. They raised fears about what a nuclear bomb in the hands of Iran might mean for Israel, how the allowed centrifuges would enable Iran to build a bomb ten years down the road, how on-site inspections were worthless, and how the United States had been bamboozled or—worse—had indulged in "appeasement," thereby imperiling its security, its geopolitical interests, and its longstanding alliance with Israel. In short, right-wing opponents blasted the Obama administration for having given away too much.

As Machiavelli knew, important political treaties of this sort are rarely needed between friends. They reflect instead the mistrust existing on both sides, along with the belief that their interests are being served. That is the case here—or, better, it is the case in a particularly exaggerated form. Iran and the United States have longstanding grievances, very different political systems, and very different cultures. But they both are enmeshed in regional conflicts that are complex and volatile. Nuclear energy was only the tip of the iceberg, though distinguished scientists were employed on both sides to reach a compromise on the issue. Especially in the United States, however, it has become acceptable to counter scientific opinion with little more than the ideological opinions of politicians with no scientific expertise whatsoever. The nuclear treaty is a complex document that runs 160 pages, and the shrill insistence of Donald Trump (also usually lacking experience in international conflict resolution) that somehow he could have brought home a better deal (naturally without specifying any new provisions) was simply bombast. Iran and the other nations (allied with the United States) said repeatedly that they would not renegotiate and that they would conclude the treaty with or without American support. After all this time, and all the false starts, the choice was never between a better deal and this one but between the one on the table and no deal at all.

The deal offered a way to reintegrate Iran into the world community. Its insularity from the West and even the Sunni branch of Islam following the Revolution of 1979, and the intensifying political tensions with Saudi Arabia and the Gulf states, fostered a paranoid atmosphere that benefited the Revolutionary Guards and the orthodox Shia establishment. Such pillars of reaction share the same provincial and xenophobic attitudes as their American counterparts among Republicans, the Tea Party, and those Zionist lobbies obsessed by existential threats to Israel. Worse, similar to the Israeli-Palestinian conflict, right-wing alliances of this sort can often effectively veto negotiations with the other side: inflammatory rhetoric, military or police actions, pressure from lobbies, propaganda attacks, and so on.

President Obama and his supporters had little choice other than to stress the heightened security offered by the treaty and its safeguards against cheating, resulting in a flood of public insults and warnings directed against Iran. The country's supreme leader, Ayatollah Khamenei, was meanwhile engaged in an even more delicate balancing act, since he serves as both sovereign political leader and the unquestioned religious authority. Amid cautious words of friendship, therefore, he and others tossed "red meat" to right-wing opponents of the deal by insisting that the United States remains the "great Satan" and that Israel will no longer exist in twenty-five years. Of course, ironically, the extent to which the treaty and its implications are undermined is the extent to which both sides return to the geopolitical imperatives of the status quo ante. That prior period offered a far greater danger of violence, and turning back the clock actually enables right-wing extremists on both sides to pursue a self-fulfilling prophecy.

New prospects for cooperation between the United States and Iran have become possible. After all, it is not as if the United States has chosen the most respected and responsible allies. Even a conservative journal like *The National Interest* (15 September 2015) noted that Iran would make a better ally than Pakistan for fighting the Taliban in Afghanistan—and that the United States had made a serious blunder in dismissing the support offered by Iran's then-president Mohammad Khatami in the early days of the conflict. Whether President Bashar al-Assad of Syria stays in power following the bloody civil war or not, Alawites (who constitute a branch of Shia Islam) will need protection from the Sunni opposition and some degree of political autonomy.

And that requires a sovereign. Russia's new alliance with Iran and the Iraqi Shia in support of President Bashar al-Assad, who will now receive a stark increase in military aid, recognizes the facts on the ground—namely, that ISIS now controls nearly two-thirds of Syria. The new coalition will obviously engage in new military strikes and expand the prevailing proxy war. It also shows that Iran is willing to align with any state that prioritizes combatting terror (ISIS, al-Qaeda, the al-Nusra Front) over an immediate change in the Syrian government.

Whether the goal is to eliminate ISIS entirely, or merely weaken it, drying up its revenue sources is probably the most important (if generally ignored) element of the struggle against terror. Financial support for ISIS derives principally from Saudi Arabia and the Gulf states. The United States will have more leverage should it work more closely with the Iran-Russian alliance no matter how distasteful that may seem. Interventionist fears about Russia and Iran should not distort the geopolitical reality of the situation: ISIS has become a genuine power while, clearly, determining the future structure of the Syrian state(s) will require input from the largest and the strongest Shia state in the region, namely, Iran.

There is hardly a single conflict capable of being resolved without involving Iran: Afghanistan, Iraq, Syria, Lebanon, Israel-Palestine, and ISIS are all riven by violence and they are all entangled in some way or another with Iran. Hezbollah plays an important role in Lebanon and the Israel-Palestine conflict and it is beholden to Iran. Fighting ISIS and al-Qaeda (both of which are Sunni and receive support from dissident factions in Saudi Arabia) would prove easier with help from Iran. And there are the Kurds who, while proud of the autonomy they have been given in three states, including Iran, retain a certain desire for independence (and possible unification) that is never far from the surface. Fueled by long-standing hatreds, Sunni and Shia paramilitary forces are battling one another in Iraq, though both are targeting American troops that they consider imperialist threats to the sovereignty of their nation; it is difficult to imagine a reconstructed Iraq without prior negotiations having taken place with Iran.

Opponents of the nuclear treaty, especially those on the Republican side of the aisle, constantly claim that no coherent policy is being followed in the Middle East. No such policy can be constructed, however, unless there is an American rapprochement with Iran. As things now stand, the United States has no influence with any Shiite nations or organizations. This narrows its options. Cooperation with Iran would mitigate reliance upon reactionary states like Saudi Arabia and Bahrain that are held in contempt (even by most Sunnis) throughout the Middle East. Lastly, better relations with Iran might actually diminish one among the many enemies whose "existential threat" to Israel's security always seems to translate into demands for more settlements and more military aid packages for more arms.

But there is the still larger issue concerning whether Iran really seeks better relations with the West and reintegration into the world community—or whether it is all simply an act. Poor judgment is clearly evident among those who oppose better ties between the United States and Iran. Imperialism has never been practiced by Iran (or its Persian predecessors). The Iranian economy also lacks investment, and expectations are that $150 billion will flow into the country. Indeed, though this has nothing to do with state finances, one Republican candidate for president, Donald Trump, has concluded that the $150 billion will inevitably be used to buy military hardware. Attention is thus deflected from the obvious: Iran needs the deal more than the United States. But there is also something else. Iran is a nation with rich traditions that reach back over Hafez and Rumi to Cyrus the Great. Ending its current isolation and enabling economic ties with the West would also temper the stifling authoritarianism and provincialism so despised in Tehran and university towns. Indeed, this is what scares and enrages the two pillars of Iranian reaction: the military and the mosque.

Closer relations with Iran, better intellectual exchanges, would create new job prospects for the young and the educated as well as contribute to introducing a certain cosmopolitan sensibility. Everyday people would surely experience the embarrassment when Iran's political leaders employ stupid anti-Semitic and anti-Western rhetoric. By the same token, they might well feel pride in the contributions of their country to furthering world peace and resolving conflicts in the Middle East. Globalization would surely multiply the current flow of information into Iran and strengthen the legacy of the Green Revolution that, if somewhat unclear about its political goals regarding reform as against more radical institutional regime changes, demanded civil liberties and human rights. Isolation fosters xenophobia and, should relations between Iran and the United States and its allies worsen again,

Iran would inevitably experience a right-wing backlash. A self-fulfilling prophecy would thus bring about something that no one wants; it is to the credit of presidents Obama and Rouhani that they knew what was at stake—and dared to act.

Concluding Thoughts

Human Rights, Political Realism, and the Uses of Power

Human rights and political realism offer two very different ways of approaching international affairs.[1] Here is not the place for an extended philosophical disquisition on the relationship between them, let alone their connection with the history of American foreign policy. Human rights and political realism have their unique traditions that are usually seen as starkly opposed to one another. But the interplay between them became apparent in much of President Obama's foreign policy and in an increasingly global society. Understanding the connection between human rights and political realism is the only way for citizens to ask the questions necessary to judge American foreign policy in a meaningful way—now and in the future.

Human rights gripped the popular imagination in the aftermath of World War II. It responded to the self-styled political realism of totalitarian leaders and perhaps even more to the barbarism of what Daniel Rousset termed "the concentration camp universe" exemplified by Auschwitz and the Gulag. With the liberation of the formerly colonized world, the idea of human rights provides new hope for a more civilized world. The idea of human rights has its roots in the Bible, natural law, and classical humanist notions concerning the "dignity of man." But it was the Enlightenment and the republican revolutions of 1688–1789 that produced the idea of humanity. This was the era of the rising bourgeoisie whose vision of national self-determination was tied to the liberal republic and a universal understanding of rights. Each nation, in principle, was seen as having the right to determine its own destiny, and the exercise of that right was seen as requiring a liberal state in which individuals enjoyed the benefit of civil liberties.[2]

As for political realism, its beginnings appear in the "Melian Dialogues" from Thucydides' *History of the Peloponnesian War* (410 BC) and, even further back, in *The Art of War* by Sun Tzu (610 BC). Works such as these anticipated Machiavelli's *The Prince* (1532)—what might be termed the Bible of political realism—and Thomas Hobbes' *Leviathan* (1651). Reflecting the rise of the modern absolutist state, these classics highlight the need for stability, authority, and leadership. All of them in different ways rest on the claim of Thrasymachus in Plato's *Republic* that justice is the right of the stronger, and they introduce the foundational political concepts of sovereignty and *raison d'état*, balance of power, and divide and conquer, national interest and geopolitical advantage. The perspective now associated with human rights, by contrast, was always employed to mitigate the exercise of arbitrary power on the part of states and leaders guided by instrumental self-interest and political realism. Thus, human rights and political realism have traditionally been seen as political opposites.

"Human rights" is predicated on universal assumptions that inform the liberal rule of law, social and economic justice, while political realism rests on gaining political advantage, interests, and institutional power. Ethical ends fuel human rights while preoccupation with short-term means animates political realism. Human rights privileges individual freedom against the state or community, while political realism champions the exigencies associated with maintaining order. Leaving things at that, however, works to the detriment of both human rights and the prudent exercise of political power. Blindness to real constraints and conflicts results if the pursuit of rights is undertaken without reference to material interests. Political realists have long noted how the road to hell is paved with good intentions. Most insist that recognizing the crass reality of power is the precondition for defending or furthering freedom.

But that is insufficient. Uncritically privileging interests is just as dangerous as untrammeled idealism—perhaps even more so. Especially for a superpower like the United States, little is more dangerous than an inability to recognize the power of ideals, and the temptations of a moral climate that favors the end justifying the means. What is good for the goose is good for the gander: it is worth considering such attitudes when dealing with terrorism and events like 9/11. Bluster about the dangers of "moral equivalency" is salient only for those who have already been convinced. Introducing a moral claim of this sort also contradicts the premises of political realism. Any politics predicated purely on short-term interests tends to generate the very instability—and potential for "blowback"[3]—that genuine realism should supposedly inhibit. Reconstructing a meaningful realism, however, involves recognizing the importance of ideals and asking certain basic questions—that are still too rarely asked.

What is the strategic goal? Even with the cuts sustained under President Obama, the United States in 2016 had a defense budget of $598 billion,[4] for a military of just 1.3 million members (with 811,000 in the reserves),[5] and 800 bases in more than 70 countries throughout the world.[6] This is more than the rest of the world combined, but political realists still wish to enlarge these numbers (especially in "hot spots"). Realism with respect to serving the national interest gives way to realism in serving the interests of the military. Growth for the sake of growth can prove counterproductive especially if there is no translation into greater influence and geopolitical advantage. Such thinking can also contribute to an overambitious mindset in which determinate goals lose their determinacy. Thus, "mission creep," in which one policy aim almost naturally slides into another.

American intervention in Afghanistan in the aftermath of 9/11 was initially predicated on capturing Osama bin Laden. But that soon turned into bombing the Taliban, regime change, and then nation-building through puppet governments that lacked both competence and legitimacy. As for Iraq, where plans to oust Saddam Hussein reached back to 1991, regime change was much more difficult than anticipated, especially once it became obvious that Americans were not being greeted as liberators and nation-building was predicated on attempts to create stability without a sovereign. Mission creep has become a defining characteristic of American foreign policy in the Middle East and it has produced the image of a rogue super-power that is not only self-interested and imperialist, but arbitrary and incompetent.

Does an ethical purpose animate the policy? Confusion in terms of justifying American policy tends to mirror the practical confusion in carrying it out. That was surely the case as the Bush administration began substituting one faulty ideological claim for another in justifying its invasion of Iraq. Identified with the "axis of evil," which called forth a "war on terror," Iraq was then castigated as a threat to Israel and, with its control of oil, the American national interest. But this argument stood at odds with the weakness of the Iraq military and the fact that Iraq's secular Baathist regime was never a major supporter of terrorism in general or Islamic fundamentalist movements like al-Qaeda in particular. False accusations concerning the existence of "weapons of mass destruction" were then introduced along with wild claims that Saddam Hussein was intent upon launching them against Israel and the United States. Once it became apparent that this, too, was not the case, "hyper-realists" began talking about human rights and spreading democracy to the Middle East.[7] All of this was reinforced by the belief that there existed a groundswell of unified national support for an American presence and a new democratic order. Plagued by a confused ethical purpose, compromised by suspect allies, and without an exit strategy, the United States has consistently found itself entangled in murderous—and, occasionally, even genocidal—foreign policy actions that served neither human rights nor American national interests.

Is there domestic support? Such support cannot simply be assumed. Basic conflicts of interest over foreign policy have appeared between the political establishment and the American citizenry. Political realists consider foreign policy the prerogative of the sovereign—or, better, the state that incarnates sovereignty. It is the state, its officials and advisors, which supposedly determine the national interest and appropriate policies. Since the time of Machiavelli, the insular formation of foreign policy has been justified on a number of grounds: superior expertise (that apparently was lacking in Afghanistan and Iraq), the importance of decisive action (that has, too often, been indecisive and misguided), and the need to preserve national security (whose self-righteous invocation has been remarkably self-serving). Traditional political realists leave little room for any nongovernmental role in official decision-making. But new demands for input surfaced during the 1960s with the rise of "new social movements." Calls for expanding democracy and social welfare at home generated demands for ethical accountability and transparency for policies undertaken abroad.

Is there distrust in the government? This can vary depending on the administration and the political climate. In any event, it is not a question that realists can simply ignore if they are being realistic. What has become known as the "Vietnam Syndrome," I think, involves less the loss of a war than the lingering distrust of arbitrary and insular decision-making by the government. Such skepticism by the citizenry proved warranted given the fabrication of evidence, the collusion, the sloganeering, and the outright lying to justify any number of American interventions including the invasion of Iraq by so many in the Bush administration. Memories of Vietnam, fear of dissent, and fear of accountability led many in the foreign policy establishment to circle the wagons thereby contributing to increased paranoia, constrictions on civil liberties, and the power of the national security state, and responses like the sensational leaking of information by figures like Edward Snowden. Attempts to artificially fabricate consent over the long haul for any policy—let alone one that justifies itself in terms of moral claims or human rights—can only prove self-defeating in the world of WikiLeaks and an age of global media.

Who benefits? Calculating *costs* is a normal and necessary element in determining whether to pursue any particular foreign policy. Costs are an ineradicable element in determining what is possible in any given situation and their underestimation will surely erode whatever original consensus existed for the policy in question: the Iraq conflict at its height cost the United States over $380 million per day, the American policy in Afghanistan $300 million per day, and the Libyan intervention $55 million per day and rising. But the issue is not merely the monetary costs. Too often, political realists fail to consider the costs paid by nations supposedly reaping the benefits of American policy. Lenin liked to say that you couldn't make an omelet without breaking eggs, which is true, but sometimes breaking eggs results only in a mess.

The United States has suffered a loss of moral capital through use of rendition, torture, and self-serving talk about collateral damage. That is why supposed beneficiaries so often appear ungrateful. They are paying the highest price for the decisions made by others elsewhere. Even should a democratic state emerge in Iraq, for example, it will have come at virtually genocidal cost: a study conducted by Johns Hopkins University in 2006 estimated six to eight hundred thousand dead in a country of twenty-seven million, between five and ten times that number wounded, thousands in exile, ecological damage, and more: such are the costs paid by Iraqis, not Americans. Calculating the gains and losses of a political policy is not merely a mathematical but a normative endeavor. Both at home and abroad there is a growing belief that justifications for American foreign policy in terms of spreading democracy or human rights merely serve as cover for "oil" and other powerful lobbies (Bechtel, Halliburton, XE) and political interests. Costs and benefits cannot simply be calculated from the perspective of the United States or in relation to its policy aims. Little wonder that American concern over human rights abuses is greeted with cynicism, especially by those who suffer from them.

Is there a double standard? In the aftermath of 9/11, the United States has increasingly been accused of employing a double standard. Residues of the "preemptive strike" doctrine still exist in the use of drones and support for bombing Iran's nuclear facilities. The "preemptive strike" is predicated on the right of the United States (or Israel) to attack any nation deemed a threat to national security interests. Other nations are, however, denied the same right. American realists considerate it self-evident that their country should sponsor authoritarian regimes in Saudi Arabia and Pakistan and brand others like Iran as "rogue" states. Of course, then comes the shock when the rest of the world refuses to view the United States as the beacon of democracy. Arguably the most perverse example of the double standard, however, is that the United States—the only nation ever to employ the atomic bomb (not just once, but twice)—should threaten Iran with military action for building a nuclear facility that might produce a nuclear device in about ten years for some future leadership that might use it against us (!) or Israel.

Why this intervention? There are certain politicians and policymakers who never encountered a crisis for which American intervention wasn't a remedy: Richard Barnett called them "white collar militarists." But, then, hundreds of wars and thousands of human rights abuses are taking place as these words are being read. It is always legitimate to ask how egregious is *this* particular breach of human rights? Why is *this* particular nation the target? How does *this* crisis affect the national interest and the world community? One size does not fit all when it comes to foreign policy and the pursuit of human rights. This only makes the justification for any particular action in any particular instance more important. Indeed, what matters is less the inability to intervene everywhere than the ability to fashion an intervention in a particular instance that is prudent and works to the benefit of the peoples involved.

The arrogance of power: Arguments that the end justifies the means have always been tautological—since it is only the means that produce the end. The real question—which always remains to be asked—is: what justifies the end other than the means used to bring it about. Emphasizing universal standards of behavior (though not so vociferously when the culprit is the United States), liberal hawks no less than neo-conservatives claim that they stand for human rights *wherever* they are denied and they bring the same proscriptions into play on a sliding scale whether in Iraq, Afghanistan, Sudan, Pakistan, Libya, Somalia, Iran, or the Ukraine. Sensationalist publicity campaigns begin the process that leads to demands for sanctions, "strategic" bombings, and—ultimately—regime change brought about by military intervention. These idealists are unrealistic realists in disguise. They simply assume that because the end is pure, anything is permitted and that, even if the policy is vague, support can be mobilized. Costs are secondary because "the people"—the beneficiaries of American largesse—are always awaiting our intervention with bated breath. A dose of genuine political realism wouldn't hurt these idealists seeking to carry the banner of democracy on their bayonets.

Effective foreign policy today rests on recognizing the interplay between human rights and political realism. Principles are not neatly divorced from interests—and advocates of political realism should take heed. The United States has hardly ever taken military action against "white" nations (other than when it was directly attacked); architects of its foreign policy would say that racism had nothing to do with the decisions and yet it is doubtful that the other nations involved, ranging from Latin America to the Philippines, feel the same way. There is a blindness at work in American foreign policy that involves the "Other." Old sayings bear repeating: "Tell me what you do not what you believe!" or "Tell me who your friends are and I will tell you who you are." It doesn't help for frustrated political realists to insist that the world is a "dangerous place": not only the victims but the more disinterested parties will challenge what the late Senator J. William Fulbright termed "the arrogance of power."

Credibility is, today, of fundamental importance for carrying through any foreign policy endeavor—and credibility presupposes transparency and respect for democratic traditions and international legal norms. Corrupt tactics and the cynical choice of allies have undermined the credibility of America's ethical commitments, the legitimacy of its national interests, and its ability to garner influence. Rousseau was surely correct in *The Social Contract* (1762) when he noted, "The strongest is never strong enough to be always the master, unless he transforms strength into right, and obedience into duty."

Admittedly, the connection between human rights and political realism (or between ends and means) can never prove *absolute*: to demand that is utopian. But it is legitimate to ask of policymakers that they demonstrate a *plausible* connection between principles and interests in the policies they propose. Determining whether that is indeed the case requires vigorous debate without the arbitrary invocation of "national security." When it comes to human rights and American foreign policy, indeed, there is no finessing the implications of political realism: democracy is what democracy does.

Notes

Introduction: Obama's Legacy

1. Paul Waldman, "Guess What: Barack Obama Has Been a Great President for Job Creation," *Washington Post*, 8 January 2016, https://www.washingtonpost.com/blogs/plum-line/wp/2016/01/08/guess-what-barack-obama-has-been-a-great-president-for-job-creation/.

2. "Final Rule: Overtime," United States Department of Labor, https://www.dol.gov/whd/overtime/final2016/.

3. Danielle Douglas-Gabriel, "The Obama Administration's Plan to Lower the Student Debt Payments of Millions More Americans," *Washington Post*, 10 July 2015, https://www.washingtonpost.com/news/get-there/wp/2015/07/10/the-obama-administrations-plan-to-lower-the-student-debt-payments-of-millions-more-americans/.

4. Dave Jamieson, "Obama and Democrats Raise Their Minimum Wage Proposal to $12," *Huffington Post*, 30 April 2015 http://www.huffingtonpost.com/2015/04/30/12-minimum-wage_n_7183780.html.

5. Jeanne Sahadi, "Taxing the Rich: The Record under Obama," *CNN*, 30 January 2015, http://money.cnn.com/2015/01/30/pf/taxes/obama-taxes-rich/.

6. "ObamaCare Enrollment Numbers," Obamacare Facts, http://obamacarefacts.com/sign-ups/obamacare-enrollment-numbers/.

Chapter 2. The Enlightenment Lives!

1. For a broader discussion, see Stephen Eric Bronner, *Reclaiming the Enlightenment: Toward a Politics of Radical Engagement* (New York: Columbia University Press, 2004), 133ff.

2. For an interesting work that explores how thoughts about dealing with Islam influenced important politicians in the early American Republic founders and shaped their understanding of tolerance, see Denise A. Spellberg, *Thomas Jefferson's*

Qur'an: Islam and the Founders (New York: Vintage, 2013). On the global reach of the Enlightenment see, Vera Schwarcz, *The Chinese Enlightenment: Intellectuals and the Legacy of the May Fourth Movement of 1919* (Berkeley: University of California Press, 1990) and Ali Mirsepassi, *Political Islam, Iran, and the Enlightenment: Philosophies of Hope and Despair* (New York: Cambridge University Press, 2011), 157ff.

3. Gertrude Himmelfarb, *The Roads of Modernity: The British, French, and American Enlightenments* (New York: Vintage, 2005).

4. Note the classic study, first published in 1947, by Max Horkheimer and Theodor W. Adorno, *Dialectic of the Enlightenment: Philosophical Fragments*, ed. Gunzelin Schmid Noerr and trans. Edmund Jephcott (Palo Alto: Stanford University Press, 2007). Also see Zygmunt Baumann, *Modernity and the Holocaust* (Ithaca: Cornell University Press, 2001).

Chapter 5. Tolerating Intolerance

1. Hannah Arendt, *Lectures on Kant's Political Philosophy* (Chicago: University of Chicago Press, 1982).

2. "As if there were the slightest danger of too much intellectualism on earth! Elementary fairness should counsel us to cherish and protect the feeble little flame of reason, intellect, and justice . . ." Thomas Mann, "Nietzsche's Philosophy in the Light of Recent History," in *Last Essays*, trans. Richard Winston, Clara Winston, Tania Stern, and James Stern (New York: Alfred Knopf, 1970), 162.

Chapter 6. Albert Camus: On the Fiftieth Anniversary of His Death

1. For a more extensive discussion, see Stephen Eric Bronner, *Camus: Portrait of a Moralist* (Chicago: University of Chicago Press, 2009).

Chapter 9. Gaza on My Mind: Old Hopes, Mistaken Assumptions, and New Ideas on the Israeli-Palestinian Conflict

1. Note the excellent discussion by Henry Siegman, "Israel's Lies," *London Review of Books*, 28 January 28 2009, http://www.lrb.co.uk/v31/n02/henry-siegman/israels-lies.

2. See my essay, "Withdrawal Pains: Gaza, Peace, and the Future of Palestine," originally published in 2005, included in *Peace Out of Reach: Middle Eastern Travels and the Search for Reconciliation*, ed. Stephen Eric Bronner (Lexington: University Press of Kentucky, 2007), 75ff.

3. Stephen Eric Bronner, "Who Are the Palestinians Today?" *Logos: A Journal of Modern Society and Culture* 7.1 (2008).

4. Avi Shlaim, "How Israel Brought Gaza to the Brink of Humanitarian Catastrophe," *The Guardian* (7 January 2009).

5. Note the discussion in Stephen Eric Bronner, "States of Despair: History, Politics, and the Struggle for Palestine," in *Blood in the Sand: Imperial Fantasies, Right-Wing Ambitions, and the Erosion of American Democracy*, ed. Stephen Eric Bronner (Lexington: University Press of Kentucky, 2005), 60ff.

6. Menachem Klein, *Jerusalem: The Contested City* (New York: New York University Press, 2001).

7. Glenn Greenwald, "More Oddities in the U.S. 'Debate' Over Israel/Gaza," *Salon*, 2 January 2009, http://www.salon.com/2009/01/02/israel_6/.

Chapter 10. Netanyahu's Rhetoric

1. An official transcript of the meeting was made public in 1964 by the World Future Fund: "Adolf Hitler and the Grand Mufti of Jerusalem," *World Future Fund*, 28 November 1941, http://www.worldfuturefund.org/wffmaster/Reading/Total/hitler.mufti.htm.

2. Stephen Eric Bronner, *A Rumor about the Jews: Anti-Semitism, Conspiracy, and the Protocols of Zion* (New York: Oxford University Press, 2003), 117ff.

Chapter 14. A Short Report on Violence in the United States

1. Mona Chalabi, "US Mass Shootings Becoming More Frequent—and More Deadly," *The Guardian*, 2 December 2015, http://www.theguardian.com/us-news/2015/dec/02/mass-shootings-in-america-numbers-more-frequent-more-deadly.

2. Philip Rucker and Sean Sullivan, "Gun Rights? Try Gun Pride: GOP Candidates Display Firearms Machismo," *Washington Post*, December 4, 2015, https://www.washingtonpost.com/politics/gun-rights-try-gun-pride-gop-candidates-display-firearms-machismo/2015/12/04/1f24fa12-9ab5-11e5-94f0-9eeaff906ef3_story.html.

3. Cornel West, "Nihilism in Black America," in *Twentieth Century Political Theory*, ed. Stephen Eric Bronner, Second Edition (New York: Routledge, 2006), 349–356.

Chapter 15. Socialism in America

1. Though it may seem counter-intuitive, the socialist movement originally flourished not necessarily in the most economically deprived parts of Western society but in those nations that suffered under authoritarian or monarchical regimes.

Privileging economics was less the position of Karl Marx than that of his "revisionist" interpreters like Eduard Bernstein. For a fine analysis, see John H. Kautsky, *Karl Kautsky: Marxism, Revolution, and Democracy* (New Brunswick: Transaction, 1994); Manfred Steger, *The Quest for Evolutionary Socialism: Eduard Bernstein and Social Democracy* (New York: Cambridge University Press, 1997).

2. The "class ideal" is embodied in practical demands that speak to the needs of working people in all identity groups without privileging any. Class solidarity is the obvious goal. Stephen Eric Bronner, *Socialism Unbound: Principles, Practices and Prospects*, Second Edition (New York: Columbia University Press, 2011), 145–183.

Chapter 19. Walking Wall Street

1. Linette Lopez, "Occupy Wall Street's Plans for a National Convention," *Business Insider*, 14 October 2011, http://www.businessinsider.com/occupy-wall-street-has-plans-for-a-coordinated-national-gathering-2011-10.

Chapter 22. The Sovereign

1. Bernard Lewis, *What Went Wrong? Western Impact and Middle Eastern Response* (New York: Oxford University Press, 2002).

2. Peter H. Wilson, *The Thirty Years War: Europe's Tragedy* (Cambridge: Belknap Press, 2011).

3. Anticipating the end of World War I, the Sykes-Picot Agreement of 1916 secretly divided the lands of the Ottoman Empire into British and French spheres of influence. The Mesopotamian provinces around Baghdad and Basra went to England, while France gained control of Syria, Lebanon, Jordan, and Northern Iraq. This European agreement rendered any organic development of Arab nationalism with an attendant national bourgeoisie and sovereign state impossible. Note the excellent discussion by David Fromkin, *A Peace to End All Peace: The Fall of the Ottoman Empire and the Creation of the Modern Middle East* (New York: Henry Holt, 1989), 189ff and passim.

4. Robert Kagan, *Of Paradise and Power: America and Europe in the New World Order* (New York: Vintage, 2004).

5. "Body Count," Physicians for Social Responsibility, March 2015 (First International Edition), http://www.psr.org/assets/pdfs/body-count.pdf.

6. H. A. Goodman, "6,845 Americans Died and 900,000 Were Injured in Iraq and Afghanistan. Say 'No' to Obama's War," 12 February 2015, http://www.huffingtonpost.com/h-a-goodman/6845-americans-died-and-9_b_6667830.html; Ernesto Londoño, "Study: Iraq, Afghan War Costs to Top $4 Trillion," 28 March 2013,

https://www.washingtonpost.com/world/national-security/study-iraq-afghan-war-costs-to-top-4-trillion/2013/03/28/b82a5dce-97ed-11e2-814b-063623d80a60_story.html.

Chapter 23. The Forest and the Trees: The United States in Afghanistan

1. Perhaps that has something to do with ongoing academic efforts in international relations to revise history and "prove" that the United States actually won the Vietnam War. Note the critical discussion by Kurt Jacobsen, *Pacification and Its Discontents* (Chicago: Prickly Paradigm Press, 2009).

2. William D. Hartung, "Obama and the Permanent War Budget," *Foreign Policy in Focus*, 23 December 2009, http://fpif.org/obama_and_the_permanent_war_budget/.

3. See Seth G. Jones, *In the Graveyard of Empires: America's War in Afghanistan* (New York: Norton, 2009); Ahmed Rashid, *Descent into Chaos: The U.S. and the Disaster in Pakistan, Afghanistan, and Central Asia* (New York: Penguin, 2009).

4. "National Defense Budget Estimates for FY 2001," US Department of Defense, 7 February 2000, http://comptroller.defense.gov/Portals/45/Documents/defbudget/Docs/fy2001_greenbook; "DoD Releases Fiscal 2010 Budget Proposal," US Department of Defense, 7 May 2009, http://defense.gov/releases/release.aspx?releaseid=12652.

5. John Dyer, "US Aid to Afghanistan Has Largely Been Wasted and Stolen, Report Says," *Vice News*, 14 October 2015, https://news.vice.com/article/us-aid-to-afghanistan-has-largely-been-wasted-and-stolen-report-says.

6. Emma Graham-Harrison, "Half of Afghan Children Suffer Irreversible Harm from Malnutrition," *The Guardian*, 26 January 2014, http://www.theguardian.com/world/2014/jan/26/afghan-children-harm-malnutrition-growth-development.

7. Nick Turse, "How Much 'Success' Can the Afghans Stand?" *Huffington Post*, 13 September 2010, http://www.huffingtonpost.com/nick-turse/how-much-success-can-afgh_b_714957.html.

8. "Stability and Human Security in Afghanistan in 2016," Brookings Institution, 4 January 2016, http://www.doctorswithoutborders.org/support-us/events/stability-and-human-security-afghanistan-2016-brookings-institution-event.

9. "Enhancement of Literacy in Afghanistan (ELA) Program," UNESCO http://www.unesco.org/new/en/kabul/education/enhancement-of-literacy-in-afghanistan-ela-program/.

10. Andre Fedyashin, "US Withdrawal from Iraq: Ending or Outsourcing?" *Eurasia Review*, 16 August 2009), http://www.eurasiareview.com/201008157005/us-withdrawal-from-iraq-ending-or-outsourcing-war.html.

11. "Afghanistan," World Food Programme, https://www.wfp.org/countries/Afghanistan/Overview.

12. "Afghanistan Unemployment Rate: 1991–2016," Trading Economics, http://www.tradingeconomics.com/afghanistan/unemployment-rate.

13. "Afghanistan," The World Bank, http://www.worldbank.org/en/country/afghanistan/overview.

14. Alice Speri, "Afghanistan's Opium Economy Is Doing Better Than Ever," *Vice News*, 21 May 2014, https://news.vice.com/article/afghanistans-opium-economy-is-doing-better-than-ever.

15. Christopher de Bellaigue, "The War with the Taliban," review of *Afghanistan: A Cultural and Political History*, by Thomas Barfield, *The New York Review of Books*, 28 October 2010, http://www.nybooks.com/articles/2010/10/28/war-taliban/.

16. David Kilcullen, *The Accidental Guerrilla: Fighting Small Wars in the Middle of a Big One* (New York: Oxford University Press, 2009).

17. Peter Boyle, "Greens Leader on Afghanistan: Australia Should Bring Its Troops Home Now," *Green Left Weekly*, 25 October 2010, http://www.greenleft.org.au/node/45824.

Concluding Thoughts: Human Rights, Political Realism, and the Uses of Power

1. This text is based on a speech originally given at a conference, The Changing Middle East: Implications for US-Iran Relations, that was sponsored by the American-Iranian Council and Georgetown University on 7 June 2011.

2. Note the extended discussion in Bronner, *Reclaiming the Enlightenment.*

3. Note the extended discussion of the unintended future consequences of short-term instrumental decisions—a simple example is the support originally extended by the United States to the mujahideen in Afghanistan against the Russians—in Chalmers Johnson, *Blowback: The Costs and Consequences of American Empire* (New York: Holt, 2004).

4. "Military Spending in the United States," National Priorities Project, https://www.nationalpriorities.org/campaigns/military-spending-united-states/.

5. "Personnel End Strength," Global Security.org, http://www.globalsecurity.org/military/agency/end-strength.htm.

6. David Vine, "Where in the World Is the U.S. Military?" *Politico*, July/August 2015, http://www.politico.com/magazine/story/2015/06/us-military-bases-around-the-world-119321.

7. Note the chronology in *The Iraq Papers*, edited by John Ehrenberg, J. Patrice McSherry, José Ramón Sanchez, and Caroleen Marji Sayej (New York: Oxford University Press, 2010).

Bibliography

Arendt, Hannah. *Lectures on Kant's Political Philosophy*. Chicago: University of Chicago Press, 1982.

Baumann, Zygmunt. *Modernity and the Holocaust*. Ithaca: Cornell University Press, 2001.

Boyle, Peter. "Greens Leader on Afghanistan: Australia Should Bring Its Troops Home Now." *Green Left Weekly*, 25 October 2010. http://www.greenleft.org.au/node/45824.

Bronner, Stephen Eric. *Camus: Portrait of a Moralist*. Chicago: University of Chicago Press, 2009.

Bronner, Stephen Eric. *Reclaiming the Enlightenment: Toward a Politics of Radical Engagement*. New York: Columbia University Press, 2004.

Bronner, Stephen Eric. *A Rumor about the Jews: Anti-Semitism, Conspiracy, and the Protocols of Zion*. New York: Oxford University Press, 2003.

Bronner, Stephen Eric. *Socialism Unbound: Principles, Practices and Prospects*. New York: Columbia University Press, 2011.

Bronner, Stephen Eric. "States of Despair: History, Politics, and the Struggle for Palestine." In *Blood in the Sand: Imperial Fantasies, Right-Wing Ambitions, and the Erosion of American Democracy*, ed. Stephen Eric Bronner, 60–81. Lexington: University Press of Kentucky, 2005.

Bronner, Stephen Eric. "Who Are the Palestinians Today?" *Logos: A Journal of Modern Society and Culture* 7.1 (2008).

Bronner, Stephen Eric. "Withdrawal Pains: Gaza, Peace, and the Future of Palestine." In *Peace Out of Reach: Middle Eastern Travels and the Search for Reconciliation*, ed. Stephen Eric Bronner, 756–92. Lexington: University Press of Kentucky, 2007.

Brookings Institution. "Stability and Human Security in Afghanistan in 2016." http://www.doctorswithoutborders.org/support-us/events/stability-and-human-security-afghanistan-2016-brookings-institution-event.

Chalabi, Mona. "US Mass Shootings Becoming More Frequent—and More Deadly." *The Guardian*, 2 December 2015. http://www.theguardian.com/us-news/2015/dec/02/mass-shootings-in-america-numbers-more-frequent-more-deadly.

de Bellaigue, Christopher. "The War with the Taliban." Review of *Afghanistan: A Cultural and Political History*, by Thomas Barfield. *The New York Review of Books*, 28 October 2010. http://www.nybooks.com/articles/2010/10/28/war-taliban/.

Douglas-Gabriel, Danielle. "The Obama Administration's Plan to Lower the Student Debt Payments of Millions More Americans." *Washington Post*, 10 July 2015. https://www.washingtonpost.com/news/get-there/wp/2015/07/10/the-obama-administrations-plan-to-lower-the-student-debt-payments-of-millions-more-americans/.

Dyer, John. "US Aid to Afghanistan Has Largely Been Wasted and Stolen, Report Says." *Vice News*, 14 October 2015. https://news.vice.com/article/us-aid-to-afghanistan-has-largely-been-wasted-and-stolen-report-says.

Ehrenberg, John, J. Patrice McSherry, José Ramón Sanchez, and Caroleen Marji Sayej, eds. *The Iraq Papers*. New York: Oxford University Press, 2010.

Fedyashin, Andre. "US Withdrawal from Iraq: Ending or Outsourcing?" *Eurasia Review*, 16 August 2009. http://www.eurasiareview.com/201008157005/us-withdrawal-from-iraq-ending-or-outsourcing-war.html.

Fromkin, David. *A Peace to End All Peace: The Fall of the Ottoman Empire and the Creation of the Modern Middle East*. New York: Henry Holt, 1989.

Global Security.org. "Personnel End Strength." http://www.globalsecurity.org/military/agency/end-strength.htm.

Goodman, H. A. "6,845 Americans Died and 900,000 Were Injured in Iraq and Afghanistan. Say 'No' to Obama's War." *Huffington Post*, 12 February 2015. http://www.huffingtonpost.com/h-a-goodman/6845-americans-died-and-9_b_6667830.html.

Graham-Harrison, Emma. "Half of Afghan Children Suffer Irreversible Harm from Malnutrition." *The Guardian*, 26 January 2014, http://www.theguardian.com/world/2014/jan/26/afghan-children-harm-malnutrition-growth-development.

Greenwald, Glenn. "More Oddities in the U.S. 'Debate' Over Israel/Gaza." *Salon*, 2 January 2009. http://www.salon.com/2009/01/02/israel_6/.

Hartung, William D. "Obama and the Permanent War Budget." *Foreign Policy in Focus*, 23 December 2009. http://fpif.org/obama_and_the_permanent_war_budget/.

Himmelfarb, Gertrude. *The Roads of Modernity: The British, French, and American Enlightenments*. New York: Vintage, 2005.

Horkheimer, Max, and Theodor W. Adorno. *Dialectic of the Enlightenment: Philosophical Fragments*. Ed. Gunzelin Schmid Noerr and trans. Edmund Jephcott. Palo Alto: Stanford University Press, 2007.

Jacobsen, Kurt. *Pacification and Its Discontents*. Chicago: Prickly Paradigm Press, 2009.

Jamieson, Dave. "Obama and Democrats Raise Their Minimum Wage Proposal to $12." *Huffington Post*, 30 April 2015 http://www.huffingtonpost.com/2015/04/30/12-minimum-wage_n_7183780.html.

Johnson, Chalmers. *Blowback: The Costs and Consequences of American Empire*. New York: Holt, 2004.

Jones, Seth G. *In the Graveyard of Empires: America's War in Afghanistan*. New York: Norton, 2009.

Kagan, Robert. *Of Paradise and Power: America and Europe in the New World Order*. New York: Vintage, 2004.

Kautsky, John H. *Karl Kautsky: Marxism, Revolution, and Democracy*. New Brunswick: Transaction, 1994.

Kilcullen, David. *The Accidental Guerrilla: Fighting Small Wars in the Middle of a Big One*. New York: Oxford University Press, 2009.

Klein, Menachem. *Jerusalem: The Contested City*. New York: New York University Press, 2001.

LaFargue, Paul. *The Right to Be Lazy*. Trans. Charles H. Kerr. Chicago: Charles H. Kerr, 1989.

Lewis, Bernard. *What Went Wrong? Western Impact and Middle Eastern Response*. New York: Oxford University Press, 2002.

Londoño, Ernesto. "Study: Iraq, Afghan War Costs to Top $4 Trillion." *Washington Post*, 28 March 2013. https://www.washingtonpost.com/world/national-security/study-iraq-afghan-war-costs-to-top-4-trillion/2013/03/28/b82a5dce-97ed-11e2-814b-063623d80a60_story.html.

Lopez, Linette. "Occupy Wall Street's Plans for a National Convention." *Business Insider*, 14 October 14, 2011. http://www.businessinsider.com/occupy-wall-street-has-plans-for-a-coordinated-national-gathering-2011-10.

Mann, Thomas. "Nietzsche's Philosophy in the Light of Recent History." In *Last Essays*, trans. Richard Winston, Clara Winston, Tania Stern, and James Stern, 141–177. New York: Alfred Knopf, 1970.

Mirsepassi, Ali. *Political Islam, Iran, and the Enlightenment: Philosophies of Hope and Despair*. New York: Cambridge University Press, 2011.

National Priorities Project. "Military Spending in the United States." https://www.nationalpriorities.org/campaigns/military-spending-united-states/.

Obamacare Facts. "ObamaCare Enrollment Numbers." http://obamacarefacts.com/sign-ups/obamacare-enrollment-numbers/.

Physicians for Social Responsibility. "Body Count." http://www.psr.org/assets/pdfs/body-count.pdf.

Rashid, Ahmed. *Descent into Chaos: The U.S. and the Disaster in Pakistan, Afghanistan, and Central Asia*. New York: Penguin, 2009.

Rucker, Philip, and Sean Sullivan. "Gun Rights? Try Gun Pride: GOP Candidates Display Firearms Machismo." *Washington Post*, 4 December 2015. https://www.washingtonpost.com/politics/gun-rights-try-gun-pride-gop-candidates-display-firearms-machismo/2015/12/04/1f24fa12-9ab5-11e5-94f0-9eeaff906ef3_story.html.

Sahadi, Jeanne. "Taxing the Rich: The Record Under Obama." *CNN*, 30 January 2015. http://money.cnn.com/2015/01/30/pf/taxes/obama-taxes-rich/.

Schwarcz, Vera. *The Chinese Enlightenment: Intellectuals and the Legacy of the May Fourth Movement of 1919*. Berkeley: University of California Press, 1990.

Shlaim, Avi. "How Israel Brought Gaza to the Brink of Humanitarian Catastrophe." *The Guardian*, 7 January 2009. https://www.theguardian.com/world/2009/jan/07/gaza-israel-palestine.

Siegman, Henry. "Israel's Lies." *London Review of Books*, 28 January 2009. http://www.lrb.co.uk/v31/n02/henry-siegman/israels-lies.

Spellberg, Denise A. *Thomas Jefferson's Qur'an: Islam and the Founders*. New York: Vintage, 2013.

Speri, Alice. "Afghanistan's Opium Economy Is Doing Better Than Ever." *Vice News*, 21 May 2014. https://news.vice.com/article/afghanistans-opium-economy-is-doing-better-than-ever.

Steger, Manfred. *The Quest for Evolutionary Socialism: Eduard Bernstein and Social Democracy*. New York: Cambridge University Press, 1997.

Trading Economics. "Afghanistan Unemployment Rate: 1991–2016." http://www.tradingeconomics.com/afghanistan/unemployment-rate.

Turse, Nick. "How Much 'Success' Can the Afghans Stand?" *Huffington Post*, 13 September 2010. http://www.huffingtonpost.com/nick-turse/how-much-success-can-afgh_b_714957.html.

UNESCO. "Enhancement of Literacy in Afghanistan (ELA) Program." http://www.unesco.org/new/en/kabul/education/enhancement-of-literacy-in-afghanistan-ela-program/.

United States Department of Defense. "DoD Releases Fiscal 2010 Budget Proposal." http://defense.gov/releases/release.aspx?releaseid=12652.

United States Department of Defense. "National Defense Budget Estimates for FY 2001." http://comptroller.defense.gov/Portals/45/Documents/defbudget/Docs/fy2001_greenbook.

United States Department of Labor. "Final Rule: Overtime." https://www.dol.gov/whd/overtime/final2016/.

Vine, David. "Where in the World Is the U.S. Military?" *Politico*, July/August 2015. http://www.politico.com/magazine/story/2015/06/us-military-bases-around-the-world-119321.

Waldman, Paul. "Guess What: Barack Obama Has Been a Great President for Job Creation." *Washington Post*, 8 January 2016. https://www.washingtonpost.com/blogs/plum-line/wp/2016/01/08/guess-what-barack-obama-has-been-a-great-president-for-job-creation/.

West, Cornel. "Nihilism in Black America." In *Twentieth Century Political Theory*, Second Edition, ed. Stephen Eric Bronner, 349–356. New York: Routledge, 2006.

Wilson, Peter H. *The Thirty Years War: Europe's Tragedy*. Cambridge: Belknap Press, 2011.

The World Bank. "Afghanistan." http://www.worldbank.org/en/country/afghanistan/overview.

World Food Programme. "Afghanistan." https://www.wfp.org/countries/Afghanistan/Overview.

World Future Fund. "Adolf Hitler and the Grand Mufti of Jerusalem." World Future Fund. http://www.worldfuturefund.org/wffmaster/Reading/Total/hitler.mufti.htm.

Index